This Book is
Protected by
Instant IP

The 12 Levers of Business Performance

Maximize Profit, Manage Cash Flow, and Enhance Your Value

The A-Z Guide on Growing Your EBITDA

The 12 Levers of Business Performance

Maximize Profit, Manage Cash Flow, and Enhance Your Value

The A-Z Guide on Growing Your EBITDA

ANDREAS ROBERT GFESSER

ethos
collective

The 12 Levers of Business Performance © 2026 by Andreas Robert Gfesser.
All rights reserved.

Printed in the United States of America

Published by Igniting Souls
PO Box 43, Powell, OH 43065
IgnitingSouls.com

This book contains material protected under international and federal copyright laws and treaties. Any unauthorized reprint or use of this material is prohibited. No part of this book may be reproduced or transmitted in any form or by any means, electronic or mechanical, including photocopying, recording, or by any information storage and retrieval system, without express written permission from the author.

LCCN: 2025915833
Paperback ISBN: 978-1-63680-552-8
Hardcover ISBN: 978-1-63680-553-5
e-Book ISBN: 978-1-63680-554-2

Available in paperback, hardcover, e-book, and audiobook.

Scripture quotations marked NIV are taken from the Holy Bible, New International Version®, NIV®. Copyright © 1973, 1978, 1984, 2011 by Biblica, Inc.™ Used by permission of Zondervan. All rights reserved worldwide. www.zondervan.com The "NIV" and "New International Version" are trademarks registered in the United States Patent and Trademark Office by Biblica, Inc.™

Scripture quotations marked NRSV are from New Revised Standard Version Bible, copyright © 1989 National Council of the Churches of Christ in the United States of America. Used by permission. All rights reserved worldwide.

Scripture quotations marked KJ21 are taken from the 21st Century King James Version®, copyright © 1994. Used by permission of Deuel Enterprises, Inc., Gary, SD 57237. All rights reserved.

Any Internet addresses (websites, blogs, etc.) and telephone numbers printed in this book are offered as a resource. They are not intended in any way to be or imply an endorsement by Igniting Souls, nor does Igniting Souls vouch for the content of these sites and numbers for the life of this book.

Some names and identifying details may have been changed to protect the privacy of individuals.

The content of this book reflects the author's personal experiences, opinions, and interpretations. The inclusion of any individual, living or deceased, or any organization or entity, is not intended to malign, defame, or harm the reputation of such persons or entities. All statements regarding individuals are solely the author's perspective and do not represent verified facts unless expressly cited to a verifiable source.

The publisher has not independently investigated or confirmed the accuracy of any such references and disclaims all responsibility for them. Nothing in this book should be construed as factual assertions about the character, conduct, or reputation of any individual or entity mentioned. Any resemblance to persons living or dead is purely coincidental unless explicitly stated.

The publisher expressly disclaims liability for any alleged loss, damage, or injury arising from any perceived defamatory content or reliance upon statements within this work. Responsibility for the views, depictions, and representations rests solely with the author.

Dedication

To my father, Anton—
A true entrepreneur and father. Your discipline, vision, work ethic, and generosity shaped the values that guide me.

To my brothers and business partners, Anton, Stefan, and Martin—
For your insight, checks, and balance, and our shared commitment to growing purposeful, profitable businesses together.

To my wife, Linda—
For your unwavering support, even when the path was uncertain. You've been my foundation, my rock, strength, and greatest encouragement.

With deep gratitude to God, "Blessed be the name of God from age to age, for wisdom and power are his. He gives wisdom to the wise and knowledge to those who have understanding." Daniel 2:20–21(NRSV)

And to the United States of America, where freedom, liberty, and hard work still make the impossible attainable.

CONTENTS

PART 1: THE INVESTOR PERSPECTIVE

PART 2: 12 LEVERS

PART 3: MEASURE. MASTER. MULTIPLY—THE POWER BEHIND THE EBITDA REPORT CARD

FOREWORD BY RICHARD ECK

Over the course of my career, I've had the opportunity to work with many leaders, but few have left as deep and lasting an impression as Andreas Gfesser. For more than 25 years, I've known Andreas not only as a respected business owner and advisor but also as a trusted coach, mentor, and friend.

Andreas brings a rare combination of insight and execution. Many business leaders excel in one or two areas—sales, finance, operations, or management—but Andreas moves fluidly across all four. His understanding of business is both strategic and deeply practical, forged through decades of experience leading family-owned enterprises, navigating international markets, and driving transformative results for companies across multiple industries.

But what truly sets Andreas apart is his emotional intelligence. He listens with care, perceives nuance in both people and situations, and brings clarity where others see complexity. His ability to quickly understand the heart of a challenge—whether organizational or personal—is one of his greatest strengths.

Andreas served as my coach for 15 years. During that time, he helped me make some of the most important decisions of my professional life. His guidance wasn't just theoretical—it was grounded in actionable steps, such as a 90-day plan that brought structure and momentum when I needed it most.

He understands how to prioritize what truly matters—faith, family, career, wellness, and financial health—and he's helped me do the same in my own life.

Some people are natural givers. Andreas is one of them. He lives with purpose and has a unique calling to help others rise to theirs. Whether he is advising a business owner, building a leadership team, or guiding someone through a personal crossroads, he shows up with wisdom, humility, and the intention to make a lasting impact.

The 12 Levers of Business Performance is more than a framework—it's the distillation of a lifetime of hard-earned experience, shared generously. This book offers a practical and strategic roadmap for business owners who want to maximize the value of their companies—not just for a sale or transition, but for the long-term health and legacy of the business.

I can say with confidence that the principles in this book work. I've lived them. I've benefited from them.

And any business leader who reads this book with intention will, too.

—Richard Eck
President/CEO at Hinsdale Bank & Trust,
a Wintrust Financial Bank

INTRODUCTION

The Questions Every Business Owner Eventually Asks

Imagine this: You've spent years—maybe decades—building your business. You've sacrificed weekends, poured your heart into customers, made payroll when it seemed impossible, and found creative ways to keep things moving when others might have walked away. You've built something real. Something that works. And yet, somewhere deep down, a quiet question has started to surface—one that you can't quite shake: *What's next?*

For some, that question leads to thoughts of expansion—of buying another business, reaching new markets, or scaling to the next level. For others, it leads to reflection: *Have I ever thought about selling my business? If I did, who would I trust to carry it forward? When would be the right time? And what would the right price look like—not just in dollars, but in peace of mind?*

Then comes the final, most practical—and personal—question of all: *What do I need to do to get my business truly ready for that next step?*

These aren't just financial questions. They're legacy questions. They reach into your identity as a founder, leader, and visionary—and they define the future not only of your business but of your life beyond it.

This Book Is About the What and the How

Our focus here is simple—yet critical. It centers on two key questions:

1. What is the ultimate selling price for your business?
2. How can you achieve that price?

Most owners spend years focused on running their companies but rarely take the time to understand how value is truly created—or lost—in the process. This book changes that. It's designed to help you see your business through a buyer's eyes, understand the levers that drive value, and build a roadmap to maximize your company's value when it matters most.

The "What" defines your goal—the measurable outcome that reflects your life's work.

The "How" defines your process—the steps, systems, and mindset that will get you there.

Together, they form the foundation for transforming your business into an asset that delivers freedom, legacy, and lasting financial reward.

Why Most Business Owners Never Realize Their Full Value

Here's the hard truth: Most business owners never receive what their business is truly worth.

Not because they lack passion, skill, or drive—but because they've spent their careers *building the business* rather than *building the value* of the business. They've been so focused on daily operations, customer needs, and immediate results that they never stopped to ask the deeper questions about transferable value, structure, or long-term positioning.

When the day finally comes to sell or step away, the numbers often tell a painful story: A lifetime of effort doesn't always translate into the return they expected.

The reason is simple. **Value doesn't just happen—it's engineered.**

It's built through systems, processes, people, and strategies that buyers can trust and investors can scale. It's shaped by clarity, discipline, and consistent attention to the fundamentals that drive EBITDA, cash flow, and growth potential.

But most owners only start thinking about these things when it's too late—when they're already exhausted, burned out, or facing an unexpected offer.

That's why this book exists. It's not about financial theory or abstract advice. It's about *building real, measurable value*—the kind that can be seen on a balance sheet and felt in your freedom of choice.

You'll learn how to think like a buyer while acting like a builder—to identify the hidden levers that influence price, reduce risk, and strengthen your company's position long before a sale ever takes place.

Because when you understand how value is created, you can design it deliberately, strategically, and on your terms.

This book is about preparing your business for sale to achieve maximum returns for investors and as a strategy to maximize shareholder/owner wealth by improving the business's EBITDA (Earnings Before Interest, Taxes, Depreciation, and Amortization). EBITDA is a crucial metric used by private equity firms, venture capital firms, angel investors, family offices, investment bankers, and individual buyers to assess a company's operational efficiency and financial performance. It guides their purchase decisions, allowing them to compare various companies on a level playing field and choose more objectively which company is best.

Let me introduce myself. I'm Andreas Gfesser, and entrepreneurship runs in my veins. Since I was 11, I've been immersed in the business world, starting in my family's company, Trendler, Inc., a US manufacturing company that supplies products globally. Every school break was another opportunity to learn and work in the industry. High school saw me launch a venture selling surplus products from nearby manufacturers at flea markets.

That entrepreneurial spirit carried me through leading an international manufacturing business, founding a consulting company focused on turning businesses around, starting a successful sales representative firm, and developing a steady stream of passive income from real estate. My hands-on experience spans a range of roles, including transcendent leadership development, negotiating acquisitions, transforming a steel warehouse's operations, building and selling a CEO-coaching enterprise, and scaling the commercial lending branch of a major bank. I have had the pleasure of consulting for a Chief Financial Officer recruiting firm, an industrial pipe manufacturer, an industrial truck dealership, a public library, and a home improvement business, among many others.

I've been where you are from multiple perspectives.

Now, with over 35 years of experience, nearly a decade of which was as CEO of Trendler, Inc., I offer tailored business advice and consulting services to an array of organizations. I've navigated the intricate worlds of manufacturing, import/export, service-sector operations, and the subtle operational differences between for-profit and non-profit sectors. Throughout, I've learned that driving substantial growth requires innovative thinking—a truth that spans every industry.

Whether you're a manufacturing company, a service company, or somewhere in between, you're reading this because you're ready to find out what your business is truly worth and, ultimately, how to optimize its future value. You've encountered terms like multiples and EBITDA, but connecting them to your business's value might seem daunting or not as clear to you as it should be.

Before we can talk about price, we need to talk about value—and more importantly, how to improve it. Every business is unique in its people, products, and story. Yet beneath those differences lie a common set of drivers that determine what a company is truly worth. Understanding and improving these value drivers is the key to transforming a business from something that simply operates… to one that thrives, scales, and commands a premium price.

In the pages that follow, we will systematically develop an EBITDA integration strategy you can tailor to your company. Along the way, you'll meet Bob, the fictional CEO and founder of a mid-sized furniture manufacturing business. He'll be our guide in illustrating how to craft this EBITDA integration strategy effectively. Although he works in manufacturing, these principles apply to all businesses. While some metrics may not apply to service businesses, the underlying philosophy certainly does.

Goal

The goal of this book is simple: You will learn how to increase your company's EBITDA so it can sell for the highest possible price.

Simple is not easy. There will be work to do.

The EBITDA integration strategy is your step-by-step guide to increasing your company's value by

- Identifying and undertaking the necessary work to improve business operations and financial performance.

- Building a comprehensive business process that captures both the historical trajectory and future strategy of the company.

- Equipping you with the insights and tools used by private equity firms to maximize the company's value and attractiveness to potential buyers.
- Optimizing Free Cash Flow and Net Profit.
- Increasing a company's EBITDA is a 3- to 7-year process. This integration strategy will provide the tools to examine a business as private equity companies would.

Keep that timeline in mind while you read the book. Increasing your EBITDA typically takes 3 to 7 years.

Let me give you a sneak peek. This is where we're headed.

The 12 Lever Closed-Loop Value Enhancement Process

The 12 Lever Closed-Loop Value Enhancement Process (CLVEP) is a comprehensive framework designed to drive business strategy for continuous improvement, sustainable growth, and profitability.

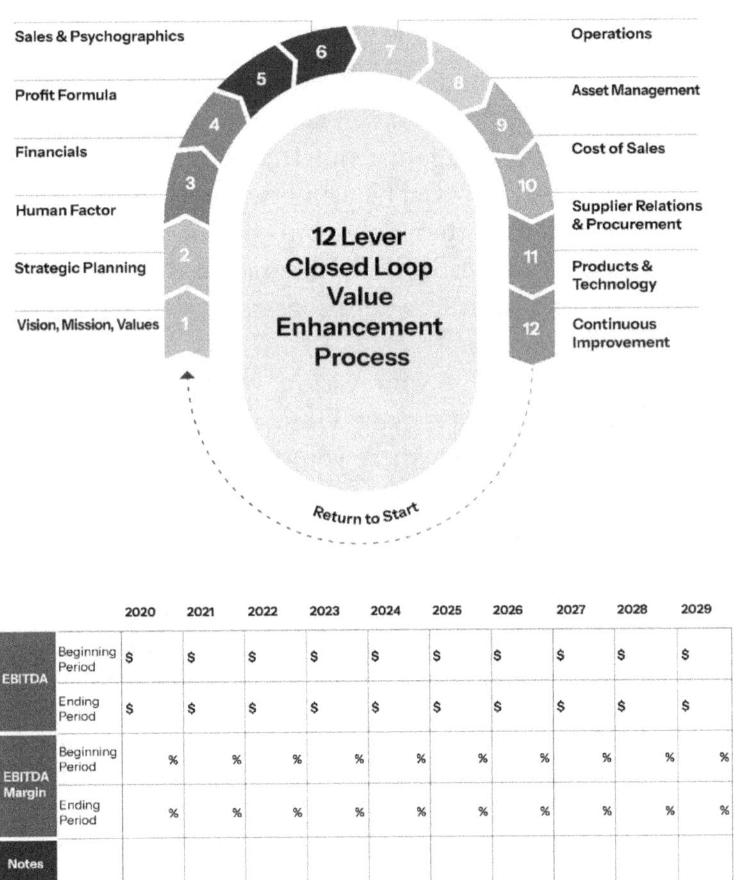

		2020	2021	2022	2023	2024	2025	2026	2027	2028	2029
EBITDA	Beginning Period	$	$	$	$	$	$	$	$	$	$
	Ending Period	$	$	$	$	$	$	$	$	$	$
EBITDA Margin	Beginning Period	%	%	%	%	%	%	%	%	%	%
	Ending Period	%	%	%	%	%	%	%	%	%	%
Notes											

Don't get overwhelmed by the above. As a business owner, you're already doing most of these. It's time to formally define and document what you're doing now.

Let's go over the graphic, starting at the bottom. The table tracks your EBITDA. What gets measured gets managed. First, start by calculating your company's EBITDA for each of the past three years. We'll use this baseline to evaluate your work. Note that our first entry tracks pre-COVID EBITDA to show the business's performance before, during, and after the pandemic. Also, highlight in the notes the beginning of your concentrated push to improve your EBITDA. We use annual EBITDA calculations to measure our progress.

Okay, let's begin again from the top. Your company's EBITDA can be improved by using twelve levers. Let's start with the big picture, then delve into the details. Along the way, we'll build your EBITDA Integration Strategy to help you monitor and measure your progress.

- **Lever 1:** Define your Vision, your Mission, and the Values of the company. These form the basis of who you are now and where you want to go.

- **Lever 2:** From here, you'll develop your strategic planning process, which we call the annual EBITDA Integration Strategy. This helps identify the most impactful SMART (Strategic, Measurable, Achievable, Realistic, and Time-bound) goals to move your company forward.

- **Lever 3:** The most important lever is your company's human capital. Prioritize hiring, training, and retaining talent essential for scalability. Assess human capital based on its potential to expand the organization and operate as a cohesive team.

- **Lever 4:** We'll now look at your company's key financial statements: the balance sheet, income statement, and cash flow statement. These are based on Generally Accepted Accounting Principles (GAAP). It is important to implement audited, normalized financials that align with your company's key performance indicators.

- **Lever 5:** The Profit Process formula encompasses every aspect of the business, from customer acquisition and advertising to production, shipping, distribution, invoicing, and payments. This ensures a step-by-step continuous improvement process that monitors progress and highlights specific areas for improvement.

- **Lever 6:** Next up is the book's most comprehensive section: sales and psychographics. Success depends on knowing who your customers are and what they want, understanding market trends and competitors' offerings, and building a sales process that attracts and keeps customers. The customer is King.

- **Lever 7:** The Operations section will discuss workflow processes and the Management By Walking Around (MBWA) approach. Firsthand observation of their company's workflow—from sales to shipping—provides owners and CEOs with an outsider's perspective, helping them use common sense rather than be swayed by pet-project bias.

- **Lever 8:** The next phase focuses on asset management: securing all essential equipment, systems, and technology. Invest in resources essential for operational efficiency and growth while liquidating assets that are no longer useful.

- **Lever 9:** Our next step in boosting EBITDA is to address Cost of Sales (COS). Contrary to popular belief, this figure is dynamic and comprises more than just raw materials. COS monitors inventory consumption, material purchases, and direct labor output, all of which are critical to optimizing inventory conversion.

- **Lever 10:** Supplier relations management optimizes procurement and sourcing to reliably leverage core competencies and provide quality products and services for business operations just in time (not just in case).

- **Lever 11:** It might come as a surprise, but we're returning to the heart of your business: your products and technology. High-quality, diverse, and innovative products and services are crucial for customer satisfaction and market competitiveness.

- **Lever 12:** Finally, continuous improvement. This lever framework helps you create a comprehensive business plan for lasting success and profitability. Re-examine your EBITDA in light of this year's events. What yielded positive results? What didn't go as planned? Let's begin anew. Increasing EBITDA is a continuous process, not a one-time event. Effective business management involves a transition: from daily tasks to strategic oversight to continuous improvement.

Improving your EBITDA hinges on these 12 key levers. This book will equip you with the tools to create a closed-loop system for continuous improvement, aligning all business aspects to drive value for scalable, lasting success.

PART 1
The Investor Perspective

CHAPTER 1

Bob's Story

The secret of getting ahead is getting started.
—Mark Twain

Meet Bob Smith, the owner of a boutique manufacturing firm that crafts high-end, live-edge wooden furniture for a discerning clientele. Twenty-five years ago, Bob's journey began in a community college workshop. Today, his business is in its prime phase, boasting a dedicated team of twenty-three artisans, as well as administrative and sales teams, and pulling in an impressive $5.3 million in gross annual sales.

While Bob, as president and CEO, oversees the creative direction and approves new designs each season, his own hands haven't shaped wood in years. The tactile pleasure of woodworking—the feel of the grain, the scent of fresh-cut timber—is something Bob finds himself yearning for more and more. He often reminisces about the days when sawdust filled the air and caught the sunlight, especially since his friend Gabriel sold his grocery store. Bob's desire has prompted him to reconsider his future.

Bob is beginning to think more like an investor and less like an owner-manager. His business is his most significant asset, one that exceeds the value of his home and retirement savings, but he realizes he needs some guidance. He's unsure of his company's value and wants to know whether there are steps he can take to prepare it for sale, if he so desires.

Bob's goal is to maximize the value of his largest asset, his business, for a substantial return on the "sweat equity" he has invested. While closely tracking his company's EBITDA, he seeks strategies to stabilize and increase it before selling, or to be in the best position to sell, or to have a company he knows is generating optimal value.

This book addresses the "How" question referenced earlier. It's about preparing your business for sale by maximizing returns, often requiring a long-term strategy of three to seven years, with five years being the typical duration.

Within this integration strategy, you'll find an outline of specific, actionable steps to grow your business's value using my Entrepreneurial Profit Formula. The formula uses 12 Value Levers applicable across all industries, not only manufacturing.

Bob's using these 12 Value Levers to craft his own blueprint for value creation, called the EBITDA integration strategy, which documents his historical performance and future strategies to enhance his business valuation.

---

12 Value Levers

The 12 key areas that influence EBITDA and serve as critical levers for value creation are:

1. Vision, Mission, Values
2. Strategic Planning
3. The Human Factor
4. Financial Statements
5. Profit Process Formula
6. Sales and Psychographics

> 7. Operations
> 8. Asset Management
> 9. Cost of Sales
> 10. Supplier Relations and Procurement
> 11. Products, Services, and Technology
> 12. Continuous Improvement

By focusing on these levers—perhaps the most important one or two at a time—Bob will gain new insights into each area. He will dissect the broader picture to better understand the individual elements of his business.

The ultimate aim for Bob, and for any business owner, is to build a self-sustaining, self-running entity that can remain at perpetual prime (Renewal/Rebirth) without him or any of the senior leadership. Bob wants to spend 80 percent of his time working "on" the business rather than "in" it. Initially, this means juggling both strategic development and daily operations, but gradually delegating to shift the focus to strategic levers. This balance serves as the starting point for optimizing EBITDA, maximizing the business's sale value, and achieving wealth maximization.

Achieving sustained EBITDA growth requires careful, strategic planning. Activating each value lever requires a multifaceted approach and may span several months to three years, depending on the business, the owner's commitment, and the team's effectiveness.

CHAPTER 2

The Conductor

The conductor of an orchestra doesn't make a sound.
He depends, for his power, on his ability
to make other people powerful.
—Benjamin Zander

It is important to have a clear perception of the leader's role in running the business. A seasoned business owner who has moved beyond the phase of doing everything to manage a self-sustaining organization can be likened to a conductor. Just as an orchestra conductor guides musicians through the stages of a musical composition, a company president navigates the organization through the narrative arcs of business, leading with vision, direction, and adaptability to achieve success.

The conductor doesn't play individual instruments like the trombone, drums, or violin. Instead, the owner orchestrates the business's various components—sales, management, operations, and finance. While technically an orchestra can function without a conductor, it greatly benefits from the creative and innovative direction a conductor provides.

The conductor's perspective is unique because they see the entire orchestra and can assign tasks accordingly. For instance, the conductor might encourage the trombonist to add more "flair" to their performance while advising the violinist to take a step back. The point is that even with the world's greatest violinist in your orchestra, true beauty emerges when you focus on the harmonious collaboration of all the instruments.

The ultimate goal of the conductor is to create a captivating performance that garners thunderous applause and standing ovations. It's not about showcasing any single musician or the conductor's individual prowess; it's about the collective effort aimed at inspiring the audience to break into applause.

When the conductor succeeds and receives more applause and standing ovations, they don't rest on their laurels. Instead, they set a stretch goal: two encore performances. Most symphonies rarely receive encore requests, and some even choose not to honor them. However, our conductor sets a high bar for the orchestra.

Imagine if management agrees to grant each musician a bonus from the proceeds when they receive two encore requests. To sweeten the deal further, the conductor selects a piece linked to the next concert's theme and offers a 25 percent discount on tickets to anyone in the audience who buys them while still in the theater.

This strategy accomplishes several vital objectives.

- **Building the Orchestra's Fan Base:** It increases the orchestra's popularity among the audience.
- **Ensuring Team Satisfaction:** It keeps the musicians engaged and content with management.
- **Promoting Future Shows:** It helps promote upcoming concerts, boosting audience attendance and revenue.

This analogy beautifully mirrors what a mature business looks like. In this scenario, management serves as the guiding force, setting both regular goals and stretch objectives.

Importantly, management doesn't need to be present for day-to-day operations; the business owner serves as the conductor, overseeing the bigger picture. They define the company's objectives by considering factors such as human capital optimization, finances, operations, cost of sales, products and technology, marketing, and competition.

CHAPTER 3

Earnings Before Interest, Taxes, Depreciation, and Amortization

If you can't measure it, you can't improve it.
—Peter Drucker

Note: Net profit, free cash flow, and EBITDA (Earnings Before Interest, Taxes, Depreciation, and Amortization) are three interconnected metrics for evaluating a company's performance. Net profit is a company's total earnings after all expenses, including taxes, interest, and depreciation. Free cash flow represents the actual cash generated after capital expenditure, reflecting a company's true financial health. Both are crucial and core elements of EBITDA. EBITDA is a non-Generally Accepted Accounting Principles (non-GAAP) metric that estimates operating profitability by excluding non-cash and financing costs.

While EBITDA doesn't account for all expenses, it is useful for more objectively comparing companies within the same industry, as it removes differences in capital structure and accounting practices.

Running a business often involves dealing with challenges and disagreements, especially when there are multiple decision-makers. Bob and his partners realized that to avoid conflicts and make better decisions, they needed to focus on the most important numbers. They found that normalized EBITDA was the most effective metric for decision-making. By focusing on EBITDA, they ensured that business decisions were based on solid financial data, rather than personal opinions or office politics.

So far, we have generally introduced EBITDA very broadly. Now, let's dive deeper into understanding each of its components. EBITDA is a measure of a company's performance based on its core business activities without considering interest expenses, taxes, depreciation, and amortization.

- **Earnings:** The profit a company makes from its regular business activities. Earnings, often referred to as net income or profit, are calculated by subtracting all expenses from total revenue. Optimized earnings is one of the most critical metrics to grow.

Earnings (Net Income) = Total Revenue − Total Expenses

- **Interest:** The fee for borrowing money. When calculating EBITDA, we exclude interest expenses to determine the company's profit before paying for its loans. This helps us understand the company's earnings without considering its debt costs. Contrary to the priorities of lending institutions, eliminating debt and financing projects through self-sufficiency are the ultimate business objectives.

- **Taxes:** Payments made to the government based on earnings. EBITDA excludes these tax payments to focus on the company's earnings before considering what it owes to the government. Minimizing tax obligations with professional tax strategies leverages scarce resources to grow.

- **Depreciation:** The reduction in the value of physical assets over time, such as machines or buildings. Companies spread out the cost of these assets over several years to reflect their useful lifespan. EBITDA adds back depreciation because it's a non-cash expense, meaning it doesn't involve actual money leaving the company. Regardless, generating a significant return on investment from assets is key.

- **Amortization:** Similar to depreciation, but applied to intangible assets such as patents or trademarks. The cost of these assets is spread out over their useful lives. EBITDA adds it back to earnings because it's also a non-cash expense. Intangible assets can be the secret to explosive growth today, for example, think branding and intellectual property.

EBITDA provides investors and analysts with a clearer view of how much money the company is making from its regular operations without the influence of financial and accounting factors that can vary significantly across companies. Ultimately, it allows for clearer comparisons among companies in similar industries, enabling more effective comparisons and helping pick a winner.

Before we delve deeper into EBITDA, let's take a moment to discuss Cash Flow, which illustrates the inflow and outflow of money when evaluating a business's viability.

Cash Flow

EBITDA is crucial for evaluating a business's profitability and operational success, while cash flow is the net amount of cash entering and leaving a company. It includes all cash inflows and outflows from operations, investing, and financing activities. Cash flow is a critical measure of a company's liquidity and its ability to generate sufficient cash to meet its obligations, invest in its business, and return money to shareholders.

Free cash flow excludes interest, financing, and capital expenditures to provide a clear view of what a company has left to pay dividends, reduce debt, reinvest in the business, and distribute to shareholders. Maximizing net "free" cash flow should be a major priority for value optimization.

Capital Expenditures (CapEx) are large, one-time investments in equipment, property, and vehicles. These are essential resources critical to sustaining operations and generating future revenue. Without subtracting CapEx, the cash flow would overstate the funds actually available for discretionary use.

Keeping a close eye on cash flow with answers to critical questions like,

- How is the business managing day-to-day operations?
- Can we consistently order supplies, schedule advertising, and complete payroll?
- Are we over-indebted?
- Where is our cash coming from, and where is our cash going?

A business might appear profitable on paper due to strong EBITDA, but poor cash management can lead to issues such as dissatisfied creditors, employee turnover, and, in extreme cases, bankruptcy. The cash flow statement is vital for evaluating the viability of a business's cash management practices. With more discussion about cash flow later in the book.

The Cash Flow Formula

Net Cash Flow = Cash Inflows - Cash Outflows

EBITDA Margin

The EBITDA Margin is calculated by dividing EBITDA by the total revenue. This margin helps compare how efficiently companies in the same industry operate.

EBITDA Margin = EBITDA / Revenue, best illustrated as a percent.

Buyers, including private equity firms and more sophisticated buyers in general, often use EBITDA to determine a company's value. By looking at EBITDA, they can compare companies more fairly, focusing on operational profitability rather than on deciphering complex and often very creative financial and tax strategies.

* * *

EBITDA and free cash flow are both valuable metrics, with EBITDA focusing on operational profitability and cash flow providing insight into actual cash movement. By focusing on these key metrics, business owners can make informed decisions to maximize profitability, manage cash effectively, and ultimately enhance the value of their business for potential investors.

- Earnings: Profit from regular business activities.
- Before Interest: Ignoring the costs of borrowing money.
- Taxes: Excluding government payments.
- Depreciation: Adding back the non-cash reduction in value of physical assets.
- Amortization: Adding back the non-cash reduction in value of intangible assets.

EBITDA provides a clearer picture of a company's operational performance, making it easier to compare businesses within the same industry. With this understanding, let's jump into how to improve your EBITDA integration strategies while you focus on solid cash management practices.

Understanding EBITDA Through Business Comparisons

Let's look at three companies in the same industry, each with different revenue. Business 1 earns $75,000, Business 2 earns $43,000, and Business 3 earns $87,000. At first glance, Business 3 appears to be the best performer due to its higher sales. However, when we compare their EBITDA margin, Business 1 comes out on top.

	Business 1	Business 2	Business 3
Revenue (Net Sales)	$ 75,000	$ 43,000	$ 87,000
Cost of Goods (Sales)	$ 28,000	$ 19,000	$ 30,000
Gross Profit	$ 47,000	$ 24,000	$ 57,000
Selling, general and administrative expenses	$ 34,500	$ 18,500	$ 46,000
Depreciation	$ 2,500	$ 1,500	$ 1,000
Operating Expenses	$ 32,000	$ 17,000	$ 45,000
Other Expense			
Interest	$ 3,000	$ 500	$ 765
Income Before Taxes	$ 12,000	$ 6,500	$ 11,235
Total Taxes	$ 6,900	$ 4,000	$ 7,350
Net Income	$ 5,100	$ 2,500	$ 3,885
Add Back Interest	$ 3,000	$ 500	$ 765
Add Back Income Taxes	$ 6,900	$ 4,000	$ 7,350
Add Back Depreciation & Amortization	$ 2,500	$ 1,500	$ 1,000
EBITDA =	$ 17,500	$ 8,500	$ 13,000
EBITDA Margin	37%	35%	23%

Despite having the lowest revenue, Business 2 outperformed Business 3 in terms of EBITDA. This shows that a company's true value can only be uncovered by examining its expenses and operational efficiency.

Importance of EBITDA for Investors

Private equity investors prioritize EBITDA over revenue because it reveals the company's profitability and efficiency.

- **Low-Revenue Companies:** These can grow through improved marketing, better product offerings, and expanded client portfolios.
- **High-Revenue Companies:** These can be optimized by renegotiating vendor contracts, improving operational methods, and refining client portfolios.

The key question for investors is where the company stands now and how much effort is needed to grow its EBITDA. EBITDA is the ultimate metric for comparing companies in a standardized and objective manner, providing a clear picture of their financial health.

Relationship Between Cash Flow and EBITDA

EBITDA is a performance metric. It indicates the amount of revenue a company generates from its operations before deducting certain expenses. Cash flow tells how much liquidity a company has. The amount of actual cash the company produces and can utilize. A company can have a high EBITDA but a low or negative cash flow if its working capital is growing rapidly or its taxes or interest charges are substantial. Conversely, cash flow can exceed EBITDA if working capital is being released, such as selling down inventory and collecting receivables.

1. **Operational Performance:** Both metrics are used to evaluate a company's operational performance. EBITDA provides a clear picture of the profitability of core business operations by excluding non-operational expenses. Cash flow from operations, a component of total cash flow, shows the actual cash generated by those operations.

2. **Non-Cash Expenses:** EBITDA excludes non-cash expenses like depreciation and amortization, which are included in the calculation of net income but do not affect cash flow. This exclusion makes EBITDA a useful proxy for operational cash flow, though it is not a perfect match.

3. **Financing and Investing Activities:** EBITDA does not account for cash inflows and outflows from financing and investing activities. Cash flow, on the other hand, includes these activities, providing a more comprehensive view of a company's financial health.

4. **Changes in Working Capital:** EBITDA does not reflect changes in working capital—such as accounts receivable, accounts payable, and inventory levels—that can significantly impact cash flow. Cash flow from operations accounts for these changes.

While there are many similarities, there are distinct differences. EBITDA is a *measure of profitability* that excludes interest, taxes, depreciation, and amortization, focusing purely on operating performance. Cash flow measures the *actual inflow and outflow of cash*, providing a broader view of a company's liquidity and financial health.

For example, let's consider a company with the following simplified financials for a year:

- Net Income: $1,000,000
- Interest Expense: $100,000
- Tax Expense: $200,000
- Depreciation and Amortization: $300,000
- Change in Working Capital: $50,000 increase (e.g., more inventory)
- Capital Expenditures: $150,000

The EBITDA would be $1,600,000, while the cash flow from operations would be $1,250,000.

EBITDA = $1,000,000 (Net Income) + $100,000 (Interest Expense) + $200,000 (Tax Expense) + $300,000 (Depreciation and Amortization) = $1,600,000

Cash Flow from Operations = $1,000,000 (Net Income) + $300,000 (Depreciation and Amortization) + -$50,000 (Change in Working Capital) = $1,250,000

This example shows that while EBITDA and cash flow from operations are related, they are not identical. EBITDA is higher because it does not account for the increase in working capital, whereas cash flow from operations does. Additionally, cash flow would further include cash from investing and financing activities to provide a complete picture.

Enhancing Business Value

To get the best price for a business, it's crucial to maximize EBITDA. This requires a long-term strategy to enhance business value. Valuation isn't just about what a business is worth now; it's about its future potential value to new owners. Business owners must think like investors, focusing on maximizing EBITDA to achieve the highest possible valuation for their company. This requires a long-term strategy to enhance business value.

Valuation is essentially a forecast of a business's future performance. Value drivers are features that either decrease the risk of ownership or increase the potential for future growth. While there are many value drivers, we'll focus on 12 key levers that are crucial across all industries. These levers can boost cash flow and minimize risk, thereby increasing a company's worth.

EBITDA is a critical metric for determining a business's valuation. It shows how well management has responded to opportunities, crises, and investments. Increasing EBITDA requires deliberate, strategic planning, and implementing each lever in your integration strategy can take anywhere from a few months to three years per lever, depending on the business.

When deciding which lever to pull first, it's smart to start with your strengths and later choose areas to strengthen your weaknesses. This approach ensures a tailored strategy that aligns with your unique business, strengths, talents, and leadership style.

* * *

It's important to note that EBITDA is not a Generally Accepted Accounting Principle (GAAP). **Generally Accepted Accounting Principles (GAAP)** are the standardized rules and guidelines used in the US to ensure consistency and transparency in financial reporting. They are established by the **Financial Accounting Standards Board (FASB)** and overseen by the **Securities and Exchange Commission (SEC)**. EBITDA and cash flow are both valuable metrics, with EBITDA focusing on operational profitability and cash flow providing insight into actual cash movement. Understanding the relationships and differences among these metrics helps assess a company's financial performance and health. EBITDA is an evaluation tool; however, it is not a Generally Accepted Accounting Principle (GAAP).

The ultimate goal of any company should be to create a self-run, scalable business that accumulates cash to pay off debt and grow a cash reserve to self-fund future investment opportunities with assets that generate a positive return on investment with a healthy flow of free cash flow to eventually diversify into acquiring other businesses that can be grown in a similar fashion.

CHAPTER 4

Multiples and Potential Buyers

Price is what you pay. Value is what you get.
—Warren Buffett

A **multiple** is a valuation tool used to determine a business's value based on its earnings. It represents how many times a company's **EBITDA** a buyer is willing to pay, reflecting the business's risk, growth potential, and market position. In essence, the multiple converts operational performance into enterprise value—linking profit to perceived worth. Multiples vary by industry, stability, and scalability, serving as a quick yet powerful way to gauge how the market values one business versus another.

When private equity firms look to buy a business, they typically use a "multiple" of EBITDA to determine the price. For simplicity, let's say the range for a business in a specific industry, like manufacturing, is four to eight times EBITDA. EBITDA shows the financial outcome of the owner's and management's operational choices. Essentially, the higher the EBITDA, the better the business decisions.

You might hear that a business's value is all about these EBITDA multiples. These multiples help compare the value of companies in the same industry, and businesses aim to achieve the highest multiple possible.

Let's pause for a moment. Before you start thinking in terms of "multiple," let's have a chat.

It is not about the multiples.

Being an owner, you like to be in control. You are used to being in control.

Don't worry about the multiples because you *cannot* control them.

The range of multiples depends on many uncontrollable factors; several are listed below.

- Conditions in the stock market
- Interest rates
- Availability of financing
- Economic conditions (international, national, regional, local)
- Industry trends
- Interest from potential buyers
- Availability of investment funds
- Market dynamics

Given these variables, as a business owner, you must admit you can't influence the multiples. Instead, you should aim to maximize your company's EBITDA. This involves strategic financial planning to effectively manage earnings and operational conditions. By improving your EBITDA, you enhance the business's appeal and ultimately control the value in the marketplace.

Potential buyers represent the diverse groups of individuals or organizations interested in acquiring a company, each with unique motivations, strategies, and expectations for return on investment. Understanding who these buyers are—and what drives their decisions—is critical to positioning a business for maximum value. Whether they are strategic acquirers seeking synergy, financial investors pursuing growth and profit, or individual entrepreneurs aiming for ownership and independence, identifying the right buyer type helps align valuation, structure, and negotiation strategy for a successful sale.

Before we dive deeper, let's consider the types of buyers who might be interested in acquiring a business with an annual EBITDA of $1 million to $5 million. A $1 million to $5 million EBITDA is a sweet spot, putting the business in a very attractive position. These buyers typically look for established companies that can benefit from additional resources and expertise to grow further.

Assessing the motives and needs of potential buyers is challenging because the landscape is diverse, with venture capitalists, individuals, and corporations seeking growth. It is critical to streamline your business operations. Don't speculate about buyer preferences because they are mysterious, unpredictable, and cryptic. Prioritizing EBITDA growth and efficient operations is the best strategic vision going forward.

Buyers expect a clear operational plan from the company's managers. This plan should explain how to increase sales of existing products and services while reducing costs to grow EBITDA significantly.

There are seven types of potential buyers, each with its own motivations and requiring different approaches to your operational plan. By understanding the different types of buyers and focusing on key value drivers, business owners can enhance their company's worth and appeal to potential investors.

1. **Private Equity (PE) Firms:** Private equity firms are often the most likely buyers for companies with significant EBITDA. They bring funding, experience, industry connections, and operational knowledge, which can accelerate growth and enhance profitability.

PE firms focus on driving revenue growth and improving profit margins through innovative strategies, often involving strategic restructuring and operational improvements.

Example: A PE firm buys a profitable furniture manufacturer with $5M EBITDA, invests capital to automate production, and later sells it for a higher valuation after tripling profits.

2. **Strategic Buyers:** Strategic buyers are companies within the same industry seeking to acquire businesses that offer synergies, such as expanding product lines, entering new markets, or achieving economies of scale. These buyers are typically interested in integrating the acquired business into their existing operations to enhance overall performance.

Example: A large hospitality furniture company acquires a smaller table manufacturer to expand its product line and reduce costs by combining operations.

3. **Investment Bankers:** Investment bankers play a crucial role in mergers and acquisitions by identifying potential buyers and facilitating the transaction process. They work with companies to prepare them for sale, ensuring they are attractive to buyers and can command a high valuation.

Example: An investment banker works with a family-owned manufacturing business to find qualified buyers, prepare financial statements, and negotiate a top-dollar sale to a private equity group.

4. **Independent Buyers:** Independent buyers are individuals or small groups looking to purchase a business for personal investment or to manage directly. These buyers might be experienced entrepreneurs or professionals seeking to leverage their expertise in a new venture.

Example: A retired executive purchases a local restaurant chain and manages it hands-on, using his business experience to improve marketing and operations.

5. **Family Offices:** Family offices manage the wealth of high-net-worth families and often invest in private companies. They look for stable, profitable businesses that can provide steady returns and might be interested in companies with EBITDA of $1 million to $5 million, given their lower risk and established performance.

   Example: A wealthy family's investment group acquires a steady, well-managed parts supplier generating $3M EBITDA to provide reliable long-term income.

6. **Corporate Venture Capital:** Corporate venture capital arms of large corporations invest in smaller companies that align with their strategic goals. These buyers might look for businesses that complement their core operations and offer opportunities for collaboration or innovation.

   Example: A major hotel chain invests in a tech startup that designs smart furniture to enhance guest experiences, aligning with its innovation strategy.

7. **Management Buyouts (MBOs):** In an MBO, the company's existing management team purchases the business. This can be attractive to private equity firms or other investors who provide the necessary financing, betting on the management's intimate knowledge of the company to drive future growth.

   Example: The current CEO and leadership team purchase the company from its retiring owner, with backing from a private equity firm, to continue growing the business under their control.

Understanding integration and communicating with potential buyers requires significant preparation, as well as building and leveraging a team of professionals to ensure clear intent and avoid premature disclosure of proprietary information.

To maximize valuation, business owners must think like investors, focusing on increasing EBITDA through strategic planning and leveraging key value drivers to boost cash flow and minimize risk. This comprehensive approach ensures a higher valuation and a successful sale, aligning with the strategic goals of both the seller and the buyer.

CHAPTER 5

The Lifecycle Perspective

There is a time for everything,
and a season for every activity under the heavens.
—Ecclesiastes 3:1 (NIV)

Like people, companies go through life cycles: startup, growth, adolescence, maturity, and potential decline. But here's the key difference: Businesses don't have to age. With continuous improvement, innovation, and intentional design, your company can remain in its prime indefinitely.

The levers presented in this book are the systems and disciplines that prevent aging. They enable a company to redefine itself, rejuvenate its capabilities, and remain relevant in a dynamic world.

Ultimately, maximizing EBITDA value is about stewardship—of people, processes, capital, and opportunity. It's about creating a company that's not just profitable today but also desirable tomorrow. Whether you're building to sell, preparing to scale, or simply striving for excellence, the principles within this book are your blueprint.

Focus on what you can control. Build with intention. And always lead with clarity and purpose.

The Lifecycle of a Business

Every business, like every living organism, goes through a natural lifecycle—from birth to maturity, and sometimes, rebirth. Understanding where your company stands in this cycle is critical to making the right strategic decisions at the right time.

"Hey, Bob. Do you have a minute?" Jim, Bob's key salesman, stood at the door.

"Sure thing. What's up, Jim?"

"I just landed a new customer. I'll tell you, they're going to push us, but we're ready."

"Whoa, let's step back. Who is the client, and how are they going to push us?" Bob asked.

Jim noted the company and explained what would be required.

"Customize? We don't do customization, Jim," Bob said. "I wish you'd talked to me first. We need to cancel the order."

"Boss, give me a minute. We're in the growth phase of the business. Now is the time to push ourselves. Yes, it will mean some growing pains, but in two years we'll be making 2.5 to 4 times what we're making now."

Bob remained unconvinced.

He and Jim strolled through the office and production area. "Let me put it this way, Bob, partnering with this company will significantly improve our capabilities and processes, streamlining current operations and enabling us to expertly handle complex custom orders. In short, after two years of challenges with a new customer, that customer is now our largest and most foundational account, thus leveraging real, practical experiential learning, improving our capacity to serve others."

Before discussing how the lifecycle of a business corresponds with EBITDA, let's explore the parallels between human lives and business operations.

The human life cycle passes through five phases.

Lifecycle: The Human

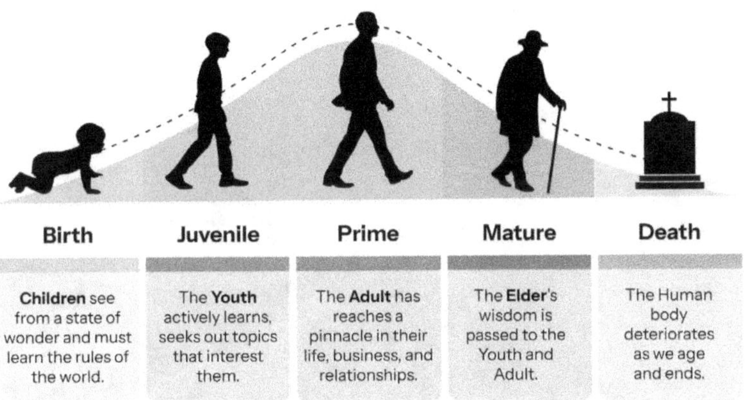

1. **Birth Phase:** From birth to youth, we learn essential skills and knowledge. This is like being in elementary and high school, where we gather the basics needed to navigate life.

2. **Juvenile Phase:** This is your high school and college phase. It's a time of exploration and experimentation. We make decisions, sometimes without all the information, and learn what works and what doesn't.

3. **Prime Phase:** Here, we start applying what we've learned. We make deliberate choices about our careers and life paths, setting goals and working towards them.

4. **Mature Phase:** This is when we reach the height of our achievements. We might start thinking about new directions or even winding down some activities.

5. **Death Phase:** Eventually, our physical bodies wear out. The duration of each phase can vary depending

on health, attitude, and other factors, but everyone goes through this cycle.

Similarly, businesses proceed through four to five stages. I note four to five because businesses have more control and can stay at perpetual prime long beyond the human lifecycle.

Lifecycle: Business

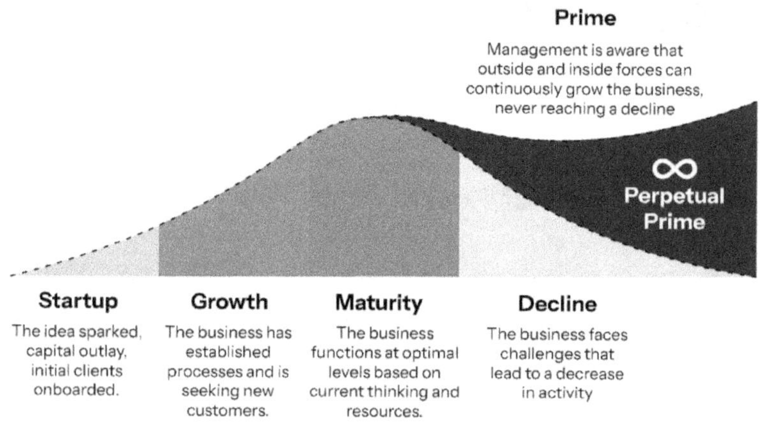

1. **Startup Phase:** The birth of a business. Just as a baby does, a new business requires a lot of care, attention, and learning. EBITDA is just a vision/goal/idea at this phase.

2. **Growth Phase:** During this phase, a business begins to expand rapidly, much like a teenager growing and exploring new things. EBITDA is a tool for determining whether growth is truly working in this phase.

3. **Maturity Phase:** The business is now established and operating at its best, applying all the lessons learned to maximize success. EBITDA is a primary driving metric in this phase.

4. **Decline Phase:** Eventually, a business may face challenges that lead to a decrease in activity, akin to the aging process in humans. EBITDA is being ignored in this phase.

5. **Prime Phase:** Management actively assesses both internal and external conditions, making strategic changes to enable continuous growth and profitability. EBITDA is a primary metric for assessing effectiveness in this phase.

Both humans and businesses experience growth, adaptation, and eventual decline as part of their natural life cycles. The key to long-term success lies in recognizing these stages and planning strategically to sustain peak performance. While decline is inevitable in human life, businesses have the unique ability to renew themselves through reinvention and continuous improvement. By maintaining strategic focus, managing internal operations effectively, and adapting to external changes, an organization can achieve perpetual prime—remaining resilient, relevant, and capable of sustained growth.

By understanding these stages—both in life and in business—we can better prepare for each phase and make informed decisions that lead to success. Having an idea of which phase you are in will provide valuable insight into how to navigate the next phase.

The Start-Up Phase

The startup phase is exhilarating. It's the wide-eyed curiosity of a young learner—the moment you see possibility everywhere and sleep becomes optional because the idea won't leave you alone. You wake up with a spark of inspiration, and before you know it, you're sketching on napkins, making phone calls, and sharing your vision with anyone who will listen.

Every entrepreneur starts here in the space between belief and uncertainty. Whether it's a revolutionary manufacturing process that will reshape how furniture is made, a new way to serve a niche market, or a boutique concept built on craftsmanship and care, this phase is fueled by energy, optimism, and risk. The early advisors and friends you share it with—the ones who see the same glimmer of potential you do—become your first audience, your encouragers, and sometimes, your reality check.

Take Airbnb, for example. Before it became a global giant, it began with two young founders in San Francisco who couldn't pay their rent. They decided to rent out air mattresses in their apartment during a local conference— offering guests not just a place to stay, but breakfast and a bit of conversation. What started as a creative stopgap quickly turned into an idea that would transform how the world travels.

Just as Bob began his own journey in a small workshop, handcrafting furniture without realizing the magnitude of what he was building, every great company begins in this same fragile yet fertile ground. The startup phase is less about perfection and more about possibility—testing ideas, embracing mistakes, and learning how to bring something new into the world.

It's messy, unpredictable, and often uncomfortable. But it's also pure magic. Because in these early moments, before the spreadsheets and the structure, you're not just building a business—you're building belief. And belief, when nurtured with persistence and purpose, becomes the seed from which extraordinary companies grow.

Bob's business was a startup before he knew it. His friends and family covered the cost of the wood, but not his time and design. Rave reviews, dinner parties, and college get-togethers around a "Bob's live-edge table" moved his hobby into a startup. He proved the idea, earned an outstanding reputation, and built an early capital system of taking deposits to pay for the wood and then collecting a final payment.

This stage is marked by several key learning areas.

- **Idea Generation and Enthusiasm:** At the heart of the startup phase lies the conception of a unique idea—whether a new manufacturing method, service, or product. This period is defined by creativity, ambition, and eagerness to share your vision with those close to you, often garnering their support and enthusiasm.

- **Validation and Early Development:** This phase emphasizes the importance of starting small to validate your concept. Drawing parallels from the early days of Airbnb, it illustrates how initial ideas, shared with friends and family, can evolve from modest beginnings into fully operational businesses. The key is to demonstrate the feasibility of your idea through practical implementation and initial customer feedback.

- **Building Foundations:** The startup phase is crucial for laying the groundwork of your business. This stage involves not just proving your concept but also establishing the basic financial and operational structures that will support future growth. For instance, securing initial funding through deposits or early sales can be instrumental in financing your venture.

- **Customer Engagement:** Integral to this phase is the focus on cultivating customer relationships one at a time. This slow-and-steady approach to building a customer base emphasizes personalized engagement and learning from early adopters.

The startup phase is a period of intense learning, idea validation, foundational development, and the beginning of customer engagement, all driven by the initial spark of an innovative idea.

The Growth Phase: Navigating Frenetic Expansion

A business in the Growth phase often experiences a whirlwind of activity. More clients naturally start coming in, and the challenge becomes keeping up with the increasing workload. Processes are often cobbled together on the fly to meet immediate needs, with little foresight for the future.

For example, imagine Maggie, the owner of a boutique upholstery and furniture restoration service. After years of honing her craft, she finally experiences a surge in demand — local designers, restaurants, and homeowners all want her work. Encouraged by the momentum, she expands her offerings: custom banquette seating for cafés, chair reupholstery for hotels, and even on-site touch-up services for commercial clients.

Revenue soars, but so does complexity. Maggie finds herself working longer hours, juggling more projects than ever, and hiring help faster than she can train them. Amid the frenzy, deadlines slip. A few loyal clients drift away, frustrated by delays. Yet Maggie's optimism remains unshaken. She invests in a new website showcasing her latest designs, launches a social-media campaign to attract new customers, and adopts digital scheduling tools to streamline production.

This is the essence of the growth phase—exhilarating yet exhausting. Every success breeds new ideas; every idea spawns new challenges. Some stick, others fail. The trick is learning which opportunities to pursue and which to pause. Growth, after all, doesn't just test your business model—it tests your discipline, focus, and endurance.

This phase is similar to the exploratory and experimental years of high school and college, much like the growth phase many startups experience.

For Airbnb, the growth phase involved significantly expanding its platform. As more hosts and travelers joined, Airbnb faced various challenges, including ensuring listing quality, navigating regulatory issues, resolving disputes between hosts and guests, and managing rapidly scaling operations. Despite these obstacles, their efforts to improve user experience, establish trust within the community, and expand their global presence were essential for continued growth.

During Airbnb's growth phase, they encountered several obstacles and challenges.

- **Quality Control:** Maintaining the quality of listings became crucial. Ensuring that accommodations met guests' expectations and matched their descriptions was vital for building trust within the community.

- **Trust and Safety:** Issues such as fraudulent listings, questionable behavior, and host reliability emerged. Airbnb invested in verification processes, background checks, and safety measures to address these concerns.

- **Scaling Operations:** Managing the scale of operations became increasingly complex. Coordinating bookings, resolving disputes, and providing support to a growing number of hosts and guests who required robust systems and resources.

- **Regulatory Challenges:** Airbnb faced legal hurdles in various cities and countries. Local regulations related to short-term rentals and zoning laws posed significant obstacles.

- **Competition:** The online travel and accommodation industry was fiercely competitive. Airbnb had to stay innovative and differentiate itself from competitors to attract and retain users.

Despite these obstacles, Airbnb's efforts to improve user experience, establish trust within the community, and expand its global presence were essential for continued growth. Its ability to address these challenges contributed to its growth and success in the travel industry. By continuously improving its platform, implementing safety measures, and engaging with its community, Airbnb built a powerful brand and sustainable business.

The growth phase is marked by rapid expansion, increased client demands, and the need for quick adaptation, often resulting in a mix of successes and setbacks. By addressing challenges and continuously improving, businesses like Airbnb and niche manufacturers and service providers can build strong, sustainable operations and achieve significant growth, aiding the evolution into the prime phase.

The Prime Phase: Reaching the Pinnacle of Business Success

During Bob's prime phase, they studied market needs, redesigned products to meet industry requirements, and standardized the product offering to better serve the market. They realized that branding was a necessary element to differentiate.

The prime phase represents a business at the height of its capabilities, akin to an adult at the peak of their career and health. Transitioning into this phase, the business owner shifts their focus from mere survival and rapid growth to developing a strategic vision for the company. The business needs to begin operating independently of its owner(s). It is now more critical than ever to work on the business, not in the business.

Move to a purely strategic position. Give managers and staff the opportunity to take over the day-to-day running of the business. This is the time owners work on the business, not in the business.

Consider Stuart, the owner of a successful boutique. His concept store generates substantial annual sales, has received national recognition, and suppliers are eager to collaborate. As Stuart's business moves from the growth phase to the prime phase, he views it as a separate entity from himself. He has built a business that can operate smoothly without his constant involvement.

Stuart adopts a strategic vision, such as "Triple EBITDA in 4 Years," and a mission statement like "We design wearable art for the creative woman." He plans to introduce exclusive capsule collections by establishing an in-house design group.

During the prime phase, business owners allocate time to assess the company, define a strategic vision, and create a plan to exceed their goals. Understanding the role of EBITDA in business is crucial in this phase. For businesses, the prime phase represents an enduring period of experimentation, growth, and analysis. It involves scrutinizing the business, crafting a strategic vision, developing a mission statement, and establishing key performance indicators to maintain a cycle of renewal and rebirth. At their prime, businesses can adapt to new opportunities or challenges as they arise.

Much like a prime-aged adult keeps evolving and renewing their career, businesses in their prime continue to adapt and thrive. For instance, Airbnb remains in its prime phase by continually evolving and innovating its business strategies. Here are five examples of how Airbnb stays in its prime.

1. **Diversifying Offerings:** Airbnb has expanded beyond traditional lodging to include unique stays, luxury rentals, and experiences, keeping the platform appealing

to a broader audience and competitive in the travel industry.

2. **Investing in Technology:** Airbnb invests in cutting-edge technology, including AI and machine learning, to enhance user experiences with personalized recommendations, streamlined booking processes, and improved search functionality.

3. **Community Engagement:** Airbnb actively engages with its community of hosts and guests through host meetups, support, and encourages hosts to share their experiences, fostering a sense of belonging and trust within the community.

4. **Sustainability Initiatives:** Airbnb promotes eco-friendly stays and experiences as part of their commitment to sustainability, introducing sustainability badges to encourage environmentally conscious practices.

5. **Adapting to Challenges:** Airbnb has shown resilience amid challenges, such as the COVID-19 pandemic, by offering flexible cancellations, promoting longer stays, and implementing stricter cleaning measures to enhance traveler safety.

By continually innovating, engaging its community, and adapting to changing circumstances, Airbnb remains in its prime, positioned for ongoing growth and success.

This is what we're working toward with your EBITDA Integration Strategy: Perpetual Prime. This is our ultimate goal: to reach Perpetual Prime—proactive crisis management and continuous operational improvement of the entire closed-loop process, and a profitable, growing, self-run company.

Perpetual Prime focuses on proactively anticipating and addressing challenges within your company's systems, rather than reacting to crises as they occur. This involves strategic planning for unpredictable events, such as the COVID-19 pandemic. During the pandemic, with millions of Americans stuck at home and economic activities halted, the supply chain faced unprecedented delays. By January 2022, 109 ships were waiting to unload at the Los Angeles and Long Beach ports, highlighting the severity of the crisis, as reported by Paul Berger of the *Wall Street Journal* on October 21, 2022.[1]

At Trendler Inc., our Black Swan philosophy allowed us to thrive during COVID-19. Our management team, having experienced numerous crises over the years, learned to prepare for the unexpected. We implemented a three-part inventory system: stock more than expected, make what you can, and have contingency plans. Like diversifying our market focus to include Government contracts was a clear winning strategy, because it was this kind of advance preparation that enabled us to qualify to stay open and navigate the quarantines and supply chain delays effectively.

To achieve perpetual prime, a management team must embrace growth, renewal, and continuous improvement. Key steps include:

- **Assess EBITDA:** Analyze your EBITDA to understand financial performance.

- **Develop a Strategic Vision:** Create a clear vision for your company's future.

- **Evaluate Business Systems:** Examine your business across product development, vendor relationships, human resources, IT, finance, accounting, and marketing to identify strengths and areas for improvement.

---

[1] Paul Berger, "Southern California's Notorious Container Ship Backup Ends," *The Wall Street Journal*, October 21, 2022.

- **Establish Efficient Processes:** Implement streamlined processes across all business operations—from prospect selection and conversion to product creation, vendor management, employee selection, and inventory management.

- **Create Training Materials:** Develop comprehensive training documents to ensure your team is well-trained and prepared to confidently address challenges.

- **Strategic Hiring:** Proactively recruit the best-fit employees and contractors to support quality growth and sustainable profitability.

- **Manage Vendor Relationships:** Build and maintain strong relationships with vendors, ensuring bench strength with prequalified backups to quickly pivot to pre-established solutions.

- **Foster Repeat Business and Reputation:** Focus on customer retention and on enhancing your brand's reputation to build a loyal customer base.

- **Analyze Marketing Efforts:** Evaluate the Return On Investment (ROI) of marketing strategies and embrace technology because the rate of change is accelerating, requiring a multifaceted approach.

- **Continuous Improvement:** Seek opportunities for improvement in various aspects of your business, prioritizing those that contribute most to employee effectiveness, customer loyalty, and EBITDA growth.

Your EBITDA Integration Strategy serves as a valuable resource to help you achieve and sustain perpetual prime.

Now that you understand the investor perspective and its role in valuing a business, let's dive into developing your EBITDA integration strategy to boost your company's performance and valuation.

PART 2

12 Levers

Are you ready? This is where the fun starts. We have a lot to cover. I suggest you get out some paper and a pen. And remember, it takes three to seven years, five years on average, to improve your company's EBITDA enough to optimize your company's value.

You can start with your strengths to get comfortable with the process, but consider targeting these levers in the following order. The top spots are reserved for those who matter most and can achieve the greatest good.

The 12 Value Levers

1. Vision, Mission, and Values
2. Strategic Planning
3. Human Capital
4. Financial Statements
5. Profit Process Formula
6. Sales and Psychographics
7. Operations
8. Asset Management
9. Cost of Sales
10. Supplier Relations and Procurement
11. Products, Services, and Technology
12. Continuous Improvement

CHAPTER 6

Lever 1:
Vision, Mission, and Values

Where there is no vision, the people perish.
—Proverbs 29:18 (KJ21)

Bob needs to take a step back. Despite himself, the business was growing and turning a profit. He prioritized avoiding losses on each project, ultimately shifting his focus to sales growth and increased profits. He recognized his business lacked a strategic vision; it needed a forward-thinking, over-arching goal.

Bob chose to engage a consultant to aid in his business growth.

"Bob, I appreciate the invitation, but I have a question. What is your vision for the company?" The consultant waited patiently for Bob's response.

A sinking feeling appeared in Bob's stomach. "I don't really have a vision. Ultimately, I want to grow sales and profitability."

The consultant looked at Bob. "I'm sorry, Bob. I'm not the right fit for you. Without a clear company vision, a consultant can't help. In fact, without Vision, suppliers, employees, and banks are not clear on how best to serve you."

Bob was stuck. "What is my vision for the company?"

While the company has a mission statement and guiding principles, such as prioritizing local resources and fostering employee development, its ultimate aspirations remain uncharted. Bob's business has expanded reactively, addressing immediate needs without a strategic blueprint. Success has come, impressive by many standards, but it was the result of opportunistic decisions rather than deliberate strategic foresight.

In essence, Bob has been treating his business like a routine job, managing daily operations without a clear, long-term target. This approach might work for new businesses, but not for one with $5.3 million in sales and over thirty employees. It's time for Bob to envision a future that's strategically aimed at and clearly mapped for his team to follow.

Bob aspires to create a high-performance culture where employees can thrive. He aims for a self-sustaining company that remains stable even when senior members leave. He aims to double annual sales to $10 million by increasing output, leveraging new resources, and tripling EBITDA.

To achieve this, Bob needs a clear blueprint for the future, starting with formulating a strategic vision and concluding with a detailed strategic plan. Developing a strategic vision requires thoughtful research and careful planning. Bob should aim for daring yet achievable goals within a 3 to 7-year timeline.

A strategic vision can focus on various aspects, such as:

- **Customer-centric:** Prioritizing customers and increasing repeat business by 60 percent.
- **Process-centric:** Focused on implementing lean manufacturing principles and clearly documenting standardized workflows.
- **Financial-centric:** Doubling EBITDA in 3 years, performing in the upper quartile for financial metrics, and becoming debt-free.

- **Sales-centric:** Increasing repeat business, expanding territories, hitting $10M in sales in 5 years, and becoming the largest wood furniture manufacturer on the West Coast.
- **Innovator-centric:** Incorporating new materials and technologies and leveraging technology for customer convenience.

A strategic vision is more than a hopeful desire; it's a targeted objective to unify, guide, and motivate all stakeholders. Ground your strategic vision in foundational values that will direct operations and decisions. These elements will shape your strategic planning process. Goals should be SMART (Specific, Measurable, Achievable, Realistic, and Time-bound).

A company's **vision** is its long-term aspirational statement, painting a clear picture of the future it seeks to create or the role it intends to play in the world. The vision serves as a source of inspiration, providing direction for employees, customers, and stakeholders by answering the fundamental question, *"Where are we going?"*

In contrast, the **mission** defines the company's core purpose and reason for existence. It communicates what the organization does, who it serves, and how it delivers value. By answering the question, *"Why do we exist, and what do we do?"* the mission provides focus for daily operations and strategic decisions, ensuring alignment between purpose and practice.

Supporting both vision and mission are the company's **values**—the guiding beliefs and principles that shape its culture, behaviors, and decision-making. Values establish the ethical compass by which employees act and interact, ultimately reflecting what the organization stands for. Together, vision, mission, and values form the foundation of a company's identity, charting its direction, defining its purpose, and anchoring its culture in enduring principles.

The objective is to use this overarching focus and these goals to move the company forward while remaining prepared to face at least one major, unforeseen challenge each year—known as a Black Swan event. These events, by nature, are rare and unpredictable, yet their impact can be profound. By anticipating the unexpected, we strengthen our capacity to respond with wisdom, composure, and real-time problem-solving. Rather than being derailed, we view these moments as opportunities to test our resilience, creativity, and leadership. Each Black Swan event should leave the organization stronger than before—smarter, more agile, and more unified. Through reflection and adaptation, we modify our systems, improve our decision-making, and build institutional knowledge to avoid repeating mistakes. Continuous improvement is not just about efficiency—it's about learning, evolving, and fortifying our organization against whatever challenges the future may bring.

* * *

A strategic vision is essential for any business to move beyond reactive growth and achieve long-term success. By developing a clear, forward-thinking plan that includes goals such as creating a high-performance culture, increasing sales, and enhancing EBITDA, a business can ensure sustained growth and stability while navigating unforeseen challenges. A clear vision unites all resources behind a shared purpose, providing direction and clarity for collective action.

So what are your vision, mission, and values?

CHAPTER 7

Lever 2: Strategic Planning

Give me six hours to chop down a tree,
and I will spend the first four sharpening the axe.
—Abraham Lincoln

Bob's been busy. He went to the beach for three days: no family, no work, no email, no phone. No noise. Imagine that peace. Breathe into it for a moment. Got it? No family, no work, no email, no phone. Okay.

This is not a vacation.

This is your Entrepreneurial EBITDA Retreat—a solitary conference where the sole focus is on crafting your EBITDA Integration Strategy. To do this effectively, you'll need several key documents and tools.

Essential Documents and Tools

- Normalized audited financial statements and a Quality of Earnings report.
- Detailed financial records showcasing EBITDA over the past three years, both annually and quarterly.
- A functional organizational chart outlining company roles.

- A clear articulation of your company's strategic vision, mission, and values.
- An overview of operations, sales, and finance, including workflows and key processes.
- A comprehensive product list with profit margins and sales history.
- A customer list ranked by sales and profits.
- An inventory list of materials and services needed for your product or service, along with associated costs and turnover figures.
- Your marketing strategy, prospect list, advertising content, ROI analysis, and target markets.
- An inventory list of your assets ranked by cost, quality, and usefulness.
- A brief competitive analysis highlighting one strength and one weakness per competitor.

Much of this information may not be readily available at this time, so start by compiling the best information you have access to and start somewhere.

Studies suggest that handwriting can enhance information processing and retention better than typing, due to the slower pace and increased cognitive involvement, so consider bringing paper copies of these documents.[2] Organize these in a binder with plenty of blank paper—this will serve as your operational bible, guiding you and your team for the next three to five years.

---

[2] Svetlana Pinet and Marieke Longcamp, "Commentary: Handwriting but Not Typewriting Leads to Widespread Brain Connectivity: A High-Density EEG Study with Implications for the Classroom," *Frontiers in Psychology* 15 (January 8, 2025), https://doi.org/10.by,3389/fpsyg.2024.1517235.

Bob used his retreat to view his company from an investor's perspective, free of emotional attachment. He conducted a historical analysis of his company's EBITDA over the previous three years, including quarterly data, to spot trends. He discovered that the third quarter, despite being the busiest, generated the lowest revenue due to the intense activity and tight deadlines associated with holiday season preparations.

Understanding your historical data is the first step in developing your EBITDA Integration Strategy, as it lays the foundation for future planning.

> Reminder: Improving your EBITDA is a process that takes 3–7 years. By the end, your EBITDA Integration Strategy will encompass both the business's history and its future strategic plans.

Bob's retreat underscores the importance of dedicating time to strategic thinking and viewing the business from an investor's perspective. By analyzing historical data and preparing key documents, business owners can craft a comprehensive EBITDA Integration Strategy, setting the stage for proactive future planning and growth.

Bob's hotel room is chaotic with papers everywhere, covering every surface, including the bathroom counter. He even tried working on the balcony, but a seagull decided that last year's employee roster would make good nesting material. Despite the mess, his mind is focused. He has settled on: "To transform our passion for craftsmanship into prosperity, doubling sales and profit in three years and creating the freedom to live life on our terms" as his company's strategic vision, combining his desire to acquire enough wealth to retire living off passive income with the goal of reaching the $10 million sales mark.

Building Your EBITDA Integration Strategy

In today's competitive business landscape, maximizing EBITDA is not simply about cutting costs or boosting sales; it's about building a strategic, repeatable framework that aligns every decision with the ultimate goal of driving sustainable profitability. An EBITDA Playbook built on strategic planning transforms this metric from a financial snapshot into a powerful operational compass. By integrating the 12 Levers, leaders can systematically enhance earnings while strengthening the business's long-term health.

- **Core Value Levers:** Organize your business into key areas—Human Factor, Sales, Financials, Operations, Products, Services, and Technology, Cost of Sales, Marketing, and Competition—to identify where to drive growth and increase value.

- **Strategic Focus:** Apply the 80/20 rule to concentrate on the top 20 percent of factors with the greatest impact on your business. Delegate less critical tasks to others to ensure efficient use of time and resources.

- **Long-Term Planning:** Understand that increasing your company's value is a gradual process, taking three months to three years per value lever. It requires support from your team and the implementation of Key Performance Indicators (KPIs) to track EBITDA progress and improvements.

Here's where we get into the nitty-gritty of boosting your business's value. Grab your binder, paper, and pencil because we're about to organize the essential components of your business that drive growth. Start by creating a section for each key area—these are the levers you can pull to drive value.

- **The Human Factor:** Focus on your team and the talent within your organization.
- **Financials:** Analyze the numbers that tell the fiscal story of your enterprise.
- **Profit Process Formula:** Analyze the business's processes and structure.
- **Sales and Psychographics:** Know your customers and the value your sales process offers them.
- **Operations:** Review how your business runs on a day-to-day basis.
- **Asset Management:** Review which assets are generating a return on investment and which aren't.
- **Products, Services, and Technology:** Examine what you're selling and the tools that help you sell.
- **Cost of Sales:** Understand the costs of making your product or delivering your service.
- **Marketing:** Plan how you will promote your business, identify your target markets, and identify the key decision-makers in your target audience.
- **Competition:** Study those who offer similar products or services.

These value levers are universally relevant across various industries. Recognizing both these and those unique to your own business is key to smartly directing your time, resources, and finances toward what will most effectively bolster long-term value for your shareholders.

As we work through this, we'll apply the 80/20 rule. The idea is to focus on initiatives that add the most value and delegate less important tasks to others. The 80/20 Rule, also known as the Pareto Principle, states that roughly 80 percent of results come from 20 percent of causes. The principle suggests that in many areas of life and business, a small number of inputs, efforts, or resources are responsible for most outcomes. It emphasizes focusing on what truly drives results. Examples:

- **Sales:** 80 percent of sales often come from 20 percent of customers.
- **Productivity:** 80 percent of your results come from 20 percent of your actions.
- **Quality control:** 80 percent of defects come from 20 percent of the problems.
- **Wealth distribution:** 80 percent of wealth is held by 20 percent of people.

The key is to identify and focus on the vital few—the high-impact areas that truly move the needle—and minimize time and resources spent on the trivial many. Applied effectively, the 80/20 rule helps leaders simplify operations, sharpen priorities, and amplify results by doing less—but better.

Not every value lever will need your immediate attention. We'll identify which levers have the greatest impact, understand what each lever represents, and then prioritize accordingly. Increasing your company's value is a gradual process. Business owners typically achieve around 80 percent of their objectives for each value lever within three months to three years after implementation. Gaining support and or optimizing value from department leaders and your team is a process that takes time. It's not just about communicating the need for changes—perhaps in preparation for selling the business—but also about ensuring that each modification is understood, embraced, and actively supported by your employees.

It's crucial to maintain confidentiality about the possibility of selling the business. To avoid unnecessary concern among employees, refer to these initiatives as "efforts to grow a profitable, scalable business." This approach ensures that your team remains focused and supportive of the strategic changes being implemented. If employees believe the company is for sale, it tends to discourage and worry the overall culture, and they will most likely look for a more stable environment due to the uncertainty. Therefore, run the business to optimize its value—whether you intend to sell it—by treating it like an investor, not an owner-operator. If you insist on full disclosure, consider offering incentives to those who stay and help grow the company. Or refer to these initiatives as growing a profitable and scalable business while maintaining confidentiality about selling. Regardless, use caution when pursuing value-optimization motives and consider cultural factors to get and keep employees passionately engaged.

The ultimate goal is to develop a self-sufficient, top-performing company culture where your business, its operations, and its employees not only continue to operate but also flourish, regardless of whether the business is being prepared for sale. Establish Key Performance Indicators (KPIs) for each value driver and assign specific individuals to effectively track progress and ensure accountability. These KPIs will help measure the incremental increase in EBITDA from each improvement, reflecting both immediate benefits and long-term gains.

Boosting your business's value involves organizing its essential components, such as the human factor, sales, financials, operations, products, technology, cost of sales, marketing, and competition. By applying the 80/20 rule and establishing specific Key Performance Indicators (KPIs) with accountability and incentives, you can strategically focus on high-impact initiatives to develop a self-sufficient, top-performing company culture that thrives in the long term.

Strategy Meetings

For effective strategic meetings, it is important to create an environment where members can openly, logically, and willingly confront issues without fear of sharing problems. Office politics plays a negative role in getting to the bottom of issues. Always work together as a team and address issues rather than avoid them. Evolve from politics to strategy by building company-wide open collaborative communications.

- **Strategic Planning with Diverse Teams:** Assembling a strategic planning team that includes members from various departments to ensure a range of perspectives and insights.

- **Structured Planning Process:** Implementing a methodical approach to planning, involving scheduled meetings, a neutral facilitator, and a clear agenda to transition from broad ideas to actionable plans.

- **Vision, Mission, and Goal Setting:** Establishing the company's vision and mission statements, setting long-term and short-term goals, assigning tasks, and conducting regular follow-ups to track progress and make necessary adjustments.

Bob returned from planning, full of energy and ready to involve his team. Knowing that his perspective was just one of many, Bob's initial move was to assemble a strategic planning team.

This team needed to be diverse, pulling in individuals from every department. It was crucial to have a mix of voices at the table, especially those in the trenches doing the day-to-day work. This included people from the production line, warehouse staff, content creators, client managers, and those in roles focused on the workforce, such as HR personnel, supervisors, and executives. The effectiveness of this team hinged on each member recognizing the direct impact of their daily tasks on the company's future.

To facilitate meaningful dialogue, the team should be capped at fifteen members. They should meet for three full days, with each one-day session spaced four to six weeks apart, to transition from overarching ideas to detailed, practical plans. Select a neutral facilitator, preferably someone from outside the organization, but definitely not the CEO or any top executives. These leaders should take part by listening and offering input sparingly. The appointed facilitator's job will be to steer the group through the agenda, making sure everyone is heard and that each suggestion is noted.

This tried-and-true strategic planning method comprises specific components and a timeline for their execution.

1. **Vision:** The company's identity to the outside world: customers, vendors, competitors, industry colleagues, and others. It drives the company for the next three to five years.
   - Example: "We make the defense of the U.S. homeland stronger and more flexible."

2. **Mission:** The Mission statement describes the company's function in concrete terms. It also guides the company for three to five years.
   - Example: "We train dogs to assist customs inspectors in locating drugs and explosives."

3. **Long-range goals:** Goals to be completed in three years.
4. **Short-term objectives:** Objectives to be completed in the next twelve months.
5. **Task assignments:** Each short-term objective is assigned to a planning team member for accountability, either personally or by overseeing a team. Typically, to be completed within the next ninety days.
6. **Action items:** Specific actions required to meet the tasks and short-term objectives.
    o   Example: "Completion next Tuesday, Oct. 7."
7. **Follow-up:** Compare actual performance with the plan and share the status at the next quarterly strategic planning follow-up meeting.
    o   Consider daily 10-minute stand-up meetings to stay ahead of emerging issues.
8. **Results tracking:** Have clearly defined objectives to measure progress.

By following this strategic planning method, the team can ensure that every voice is heard and every task is aligned with the company's long-term vision. This collaborative approach will drive the company towards sustained success and growth, leveraging the skills of a professional facilitator.

* * *

Before we move on to the next lever, add the following to your reference materials:

- Organization Chart
- Personnel list

- Roles list
- Three questions
    - Who are your heroes?
    - Who are the ones lagging?
    - What roles are you missing?

Keep vision alignment, profit maximization, scalable growth, and EBITDA in mind.

CHAPTER 8

Lever 3: The Human Factor

The greatest leader is not necessarily the one who does the greatest things. He is the one who gets the people to do the greatest things.

—President Ronald Reagan

Bob comes out of his final strategy meeting with his last evening at the beach in mind. He leaves his room and decides to reflect on his work, taking a familiar seat at the hotel bar. Sitting in the bar, he beckoned for the now-familiar bartender, Dave. He didn't need his whiskey refreshed or the peanuts refilled. Cleaning a glass to perfection, Dave, as usual, approached Bob with focused, professional, friendly, service-oriented attention.

"Dave, I have a question for you. How long have you been working here?"

"17 years."

"What's the best thing management's done during your tenure?"

"They offered paternity leave 13 years before it became the norm. It was great because my wife was 4 months pregnant at the time."

"That's great, Dave. I love hearing that," Bob said. "What's the worst thing management has ever done to your job or tenure?"

"Personally? They watered down the top-shelf alcohol. They've lost more money to me for that one decision than they saved by making it. I used to upsell to WhistlePig the Boss Hog IV: The Black Prince Straight Rye Whiskey, a $1,600 bottle, straight and in several of my own signature cocktails. I took two of my $35 cocktails off the menu because they started watering down WhistlePig. Like any talented chef or artist, I won't work with poor materials. And that's just the whiskey," said Dave.

"That's too bad. I'd love to try one of your signature cocktails," Bob said.

Dave glanced around the bar. Aside from a couple tucked away in a back booth, it was just the two of them. "What I'm about to do is probably... unethical. Is that the right word?" He smirked. "Let's just say it goes against management policy."

With a conspiratorial wink, Dave ducked behind the bar and came up holding an unopened bottle of WhistlePig. "What can I say? I'm an artist," he said with a grin. "Every so often, I stop by the specialty liquor store and pick up a few bottles I keep stashed here—for special customers."

He set the bottle down gently and added, "Let me make you something exceptional. And for you, Bob... this one's on the house."

Bob's notes from his first draft of the Functional Organization Chart.

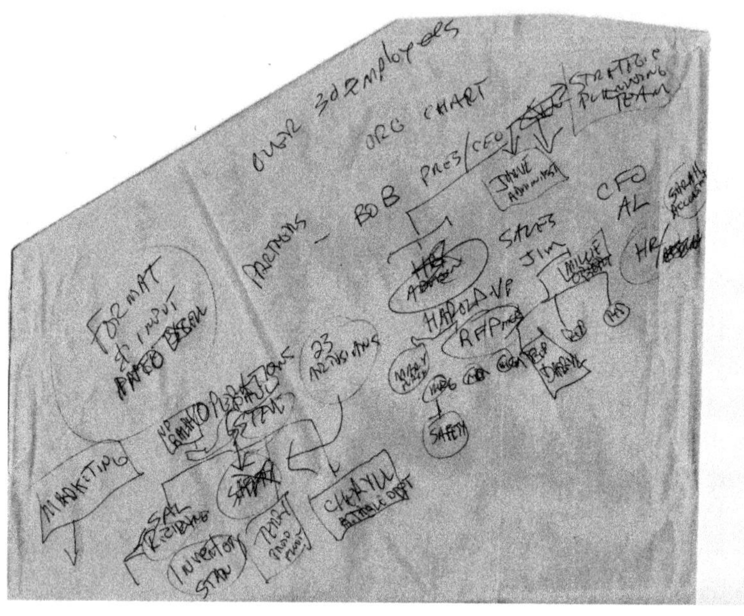

Bob's business grew with most of the same employees it has today. Among the company's most valued people was his sales representative, Jim. Lately, Jim has brought in a significant client for one of their main offerings. Once the customer's order was entered into the computer for processing, Jim passed the job to Steve in operations on the production floor.

Steve had been with the company since the beginning. As the expert on the production floor, he was eager to start. Steve was proud of himself. In record time, he produced 1,000 pieces. He advanced the piece to the next production stage, only to discover a defect. Every one of the 1,000 parts was unusable. Bob was livid and absolutely furious. Here was Steve, one of his most senior employees, and he fouled up the first order of a brand-new account. Bob was so upset that he was ready to fire Steve on the spot.

Steve's supervisor, Paul, got wind of Bob's reaction and proactively intervened. "Bob, it was an honest mistake. It wasn't intentional. You know Steve. Please take a deep breath for a moment," said Paul.

Okay, Bob thought. *What lessons can we all take away from this "event" to prevent similar errors in the future? Was a more robust quality control system required and necessary at this time? Bob realized the question was self-explanatory.*

Bob took to heart Paul's comments and empathetically approached a very nervous Steve, "Steve, I have an idea. I know what happened was a mistake. But it was a mistake that was replicated 1,000 times," Bob said. "I want you to design a company-wide quality control system. We must define all processes and procedures to avoid a repeat of this or any similar event. Once this quality process manual is done, I need you to present it to the whole company."

Steve responded, "Boss, I can't do that. I can't speak in front of crowds. I can definitely fix the process, but I can't handle the responsibility of talking in front of all the employees."

Bob knew Steve was anxious. He's an introvert by nature. Bob recognized the importance of his employees—the company's most valuable asset. He understood that Human Capital was one of the strongest drivers of EBITDA. Bob led with, "Steve, I will help you develop the system and the processes and directly help you with the presentation."

Months later, Steve's presentation to the company was a raging success. He repaired the defective products and delivered the big customer's product on time and within the quality parameters.

At the highest level, the human capital lever is two-fold. First, it's about evaluating and aligning human capital with organizational growth objectives. From there, you need to prioritize the organizational structure, hiring the right talent, training and onboarding effectively, and retaining talent for scalability.

Securing commitment is crucial. Begin with your leadership team—they have a deeper understanding of the team, customers, finances, and operations than anyone else. Their insights can sharpen the focus of your strategic vision and early development categories in ways you might not foresee. Gaining their buy-in is essential because even unconscious resistance can hinder the company's growth.

Bob dove into evaluating his leadership team to activate the human capital lever. He asked:

- What do they think the company's weak spots are?
- How do they feel about their work and the company?
- What personal ambitions do they have?
- How do their personal lives impact their work? Are they qualified for the job?
- Do they see what the company needs to do to profitably grow?

Digging into questions like these sheds light on how the leaders' underlying biases might either support or undermine the strategic vision. This isn't about finding out who's a hero or who might need to be let go. It's about determining where they fit best within the company's overall vision. It is important to get rid of people who are culture killers, deadwood, or rotten apples because their negative impact will adversely affect EBITDA.

Does Bob know that AL, his Chief Financial Officer, who also handles Human Resources, hates dealing with HR issues? Or take someone who's fed up with bureaucratic ineffectiveness. They might thrive in tackling a goal that lets them cut through unnecessary layers of management. For instance, in Bob's business, every Request for Proposal

(RFP) needs a thumbs-up or down from three managers and a VP. Harold, the VP overseeing RFPs, gets buried in them every week. Each RFP demands a deep dive into costs versus potential revenue. His managers crunch the numbers, but Harold doesn't get to see their insights on the proposals, just their yes or no. And he's spending at least three hours on each one. This is the lifeblood for scalable growth.

Intending to double EBITDA, Harold's mission is to boost efficiency, reduce staff costs, and grow revenue. So, Harold developed a set of criteria to streamline the Request for Proposal (RFP) process.

- ➢ Cut down his RFP review time.
- ➢ Reduce how long his managers spend on RFPs.
- ➢ Craft a more efficient system to handle RFPs.
- ➢ Gauge the true value of each RFP.

The company aims for a 45 percent gross margin. Before they're even considered, RFPs need to hit this number based on material and labor costs. Harold decided to cut down the process to just three checks and two approvals.

Since the sales crew was always drumming up new leads, and the company got unsolicited RFPs every week, Harold figured it was time for a new position: RFP Analyst. This person's job would be to:

- ➢ Take in and file each RFP.
- ➢ Run it through a checklist:
- ➢ When's the deadline?
- ➢ What's it worth? Does it meet the company's minimum dollar threshold?
- ➢ Is this a returning customer?
- ➢ Is it a potential new customer?

Based on these, the RFP Analyst either drops the RFP, does a quick check with the Sales Manager, or fills out a detailed analysis and passes it on with a recommendation. The Sales Manager then follows similar steps. For projects under $100,000, they either take or reject the Analyst's advice. If it exceeds $250,000, it's up to Harold, with the Sales Manager's detailed input.

With just one decision, Bob empowered Harold to address his frustrations and align his role with the vision: "To transform our passion for craftsmanship into prosperity—doubling sales and profit in three years and create the freedom to live life on our terms." Harold's new RFP process cut out unnecessary steps and reduced the pile on his desk. Plus, it gave the Sales Manager more responsibility and promoted the new RFP Analyst internally, boosting morale.

While Bob empowered Harold to develop a new RFP process and create a new position, other executives in the company view their workforce only as a line-item cost. Distant from daily operations, they may view employees as mere numbers, with layoffs often being the go-to solution for financial challenges. It doesn't have to be; most often, layoffs shouldn't be the immediate solution.

In most cases, the people on the ground are the actual experts, knowledgeable about more than just their immediate tasks. They know the ins and outs, not just the production details. For example, the workers know that Mary from purchasing is an unsung hero. She handled logistics miracles during last year's snowstorm and even looked after stranded drivers. She's got an eagle eye for spotting production issues before they blow up. Her contributions are stealthy yet extremely impactful.

The factory staff is also aware that some critical steps are missing from the new safety measures. Despite being told to follow these rules, they're worried about potential accidents, not to mention OSHA violations and union issues. The trouble doesn't start with the shift leads; it's coming from higher up. A new manager, keen to boost productivity, has tweaked the safety procedures, shaving minutes off production time and proposing unpaid early finishes for employees.

These situations are a mixed bag. You've got a hero like Mary who sees the bigger picture. You've got employees who have each other's backs. And you've got a manager pushing for efficiency. But there are clear issues, too. There's an employee ready for more than her current role offers. There's a growing distrust among the staff towards the management. And you've got a manager who might be out of touch with the actual manufacturing process.

Bob understands that effectively utilizing human capital is not about reducing headcount; it's about getting the right people, with the right attitudes and natural abilities, in the right roles on the team to tap into his team's expertise and insights and propel the company forward. Develop a team for problem confrontation, root cause identification, solution determination, and results implementation, not problem avoidance.

Engaging the leadership team and implementing targeted initiatives are crucial to leveraging human capital and driving EBITDA growth. By seeking insights—often awkwardly presented—from employees and aligning their commitment with the company's strategic vision, businesses can enhance overall efficiency and morale while uncovering areas for improvement and building a robust, solution-centric culture.

Safety Initiatives

The final aspect to consider in Lever 3 is the evaluation of safety initiatives. This includes ensuring both cultural and physical safety within the company.

The factory floor presents significant hazards in manufacturing environments. Industrial machinery like saws can cause severe cuts, drill presses can lead to puncture wounds, and welding stations pose risks of burns and eye injuries from sparks. Additionally, loud machine noise, chemical odors, and reduced visibility from wood dust further increase the risk of accidents. Regularly reviewing and improving safety measures is essential. This not only helps prevent accidents and reduce workers' compensation claims but also maintains productivity and morale.

Bob's goal to double EBITDA involves balancing expenses with sales and addressing potential risks on the floor. Accidents can lead to higher workers' compensation costs and reduced productivity if employees are absent, less-experienced workers have to step in, or morale drops due to safety concerns.

To enhance safety, consider the following steps.

- Form a safety committee.
- Set benchmarks using workers' compensation data.
- Appoint an employee safety representative.
- Collaborate with workers directly involved in daily operations to identify and address potential hazards.

While managers have valuable insights on safety, they might miss the full picture that workers who face these risks daily can provide. Engaging with workers improves staff relations and draws attention to potential hazards, ultimately leading to a safer, more efficient workplace. Employee safety and well-being are primary concerns.

In non-manufacturing sectors, safety focuses on different concerns such as mental health and conflict resolution. For instance, in office settings, prioritizing mental well-being and creating an environment where employees can comfortably and safely address conflicts are key.

Ensuring a safe, clean, and well-organized workplace fosters a positive atmosphere and supports the company's overall strategic goals.

Other Human Factor Initiatives

- Assessing the current staff: identifying growth and stagnation.
- Organizing regular one-on-one or small group lunches to hear directly from employees, mixing various staff levels.
- Conducting 360 reviews.
- Evaluating a 4-day work week with a staggered schedule.
- Succession planning for key positions.
- Focusing on organizational development and fair compensation.
- Standardizing roles.
- Linking incentives, bonuses, and paid time off to EBITDA.
- Maintaining an up-to-date organizational chart and job descriptions.
- Promoting professional growth, education, and promotions.
- Creating an open culture that encourages continuous improvement and the freedom to address concerns comfortably.
- Offer competitive pay and benefits.

Addressing safety from both managerial and worker perspectives and aligning it with strategic goals, like doubling EBITDA, ensures continuous improvement and maintains high morale and efficiency across the workforce.

A Contrary Point of View: Silos

In business, a silo refers to a department, team, or system that operates in isolation, limiting communication and information sharing with other parts of the organization. Like a farm silo storing grain separately, these internal divisions hoard information and resources, leading to duplicated efforts, misaligned goals, slower decision-making, reduced efficiency, and stifled innovation.

I'm going to present a point of view that may not align with the advice of nearly half of business consultants and managers. They tend to promote the idea of silos because they believe these structures help departments develop deep expertise, provide clear lines of accountability, and simplify management. Silos are often established to prevent different company divisions from competing for internal clients.

Despite these supposed benefits, silos can be detrimental to a business, and Bob witnessed the problems they can cause. A silo in business is when each department focuses solely on its tasks, without interacting with others. For example, Mary in the Purchasing department handles buying supplies from vendors and negotiating prices. They're separate from Sal in the receiving department, which is responsible for unloading deliveries and tracking inventory that purchasing procures. Al in the Accounting department is the third silo in this process. They pay the vendor invoice based on what was invoiced, not necessarily what was actually received. These departments typically operate independently, without interacting with one another.

- **Downsides of Department Silos:** Silos may develop deep expertise and clear accountability, but can cause major issues due to poor communication between departments.
- **Lack of Interaction:** Silos occur when departments like purchasing, receiving, and accounting work independently without coordination.
- **Example of Inventory Loss:** A business lost inventory because departments didn't communicate, resulting in mismatches in orders, deliveries, and invoices, underscoring the need for better teamwork.

Bob encountered a situation in which the business was missing thousands of dollars' worth of inventory—nuts, bolts, and lumber. These are not items you would typically find stolen, especially since the company was known for paying fair wages and having happy employees. So, theft didn't seem to be the reason for the loss.

After some digging, Bob pinpointed the issue to the lack of communication between departments. He reviewed three key documents: the purchase order, the receiving report, and the vendor's invoice. They should match, showing that what was ordered, what was received, and what was paid for are the same. But they didn't.

Each department had done its part, but no one had ensured that the order, the delivery, and the invoice matched. There was no system in place for different teams to check each other's work. If there had been better coordination between departments, they likely could have avoided the inventory loss.

Work should be like a relay race, with the baton skillfully handed between departments, not dropped and left for the next department to find and pick up before running the next leg. Improved communication and coordination between departments can prevent significant losses and enhance over-all efficiency. Breaking down silos is essential for a business to operate smoothly and achieve its strategic goals. It does require better overall interdepartmental communication and tends to highlight conflicts. In fact, many conflicts are handled by problem avoidance, which is not a viable business strategy. Progress through process improvement is the goal.

Bob's refined Functional Organization Structure

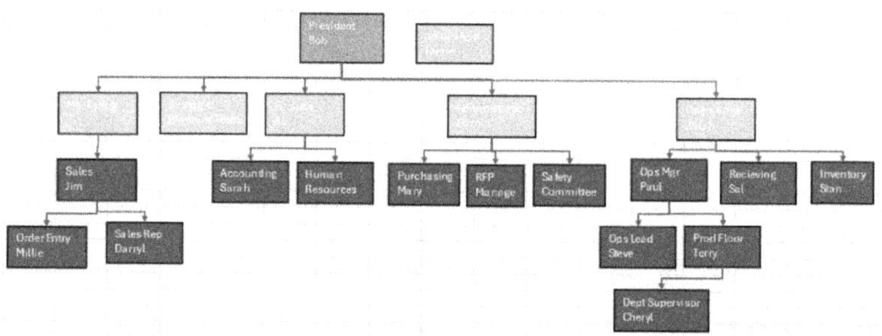

Before we go any further, this is what we're aiming for—this is our path to success. We will build your Key Performance Indicators (KPI) report so you can monitor your progress monthly. For now, start gathering your balance sheet, income statement, and statement of cash flows.

CHAPTER 9

Lever 4: Financial Statements

Accounting is the language of business.
—Warren Buffett

Financials are the language of business. To lead effectively, every owner, executive, or manager must become fluent in that language. Mastering financial statements isn't about accounting for its own sake—it's about understanding how your business truly performs beneath the surface. The balance sheet, income statement, and cash flow statement each tell part of the story: what you own and owe, how much you earn, and how cash moves through your operations. When read together, they reveal the full picture of your company's health, efficiency, and potential. In this chapter, we'll explore how these interconnected reports form the foundation of your EBITDA strategy—empowering you to make smarter decisions, anticipate challenges, and drive long-term value creation.

- **Financials as the Foundation:** Understanding key financial statements—the balance sheet, income statement, and cash flow statement—is crucial to building your EBITDA integration strategy.
- **Interconnected Financial Statements:** Each statement provides unique insights: the balance sheet shows

assets and liabilities, the income statement tracks profitability, and the cash flow statement reveals working capital.

- **Practical Business Application:** Using these statements together helps you monitor financial health, identify areas for improvement, and ensure smooth business operations.

You might be wondering: *How do I cut my expenses? Where do I start?*

This is what you've been waiting for. And here's where I tell you to wait.

Many companies think the first step to increasing EBITDA is cutting expenses, which might mean renegotiating vendor contracts or scrutinizing packaging and product stock-keeping units. Unfortunately, a preoccupation with cost-cutting often leads to viewing employees as expendable job categories rather than individuals with unique skills.

From the last chapter, you know Bob hates laying off people. Bob regularly says, "I value their individual skills, thoughts, and how they fit into the company's culture." This may sound cliché, but Bob has seen many companies regret laying off employees just to cut costs. Often, it becomes clear too late that person A was the only one who knew how to do X. These companies prioritize cost reduction over the individual's contribution to overall profit. It could be as simple as networking with new clients or as crucial as being the linchpin between operations, sales, and the warehouse. There's always one individual who ensures cross-departmental communication and performs beyond their job description. Definitely keep that person!

Instead of focusing on employees when cutting expenses, we'll base our approach on financial statements, as they are the most important factor in building your EBITDA integration strategy. Remember when it was suggested you get the balance sheet, income statement, and cash flow statement handy? It's now time to dig in.

There are several key points to consider that should be at the forefront of your mind. We will build your Key Performance Indicators report card from these three financial statements and your industry's key performance standards.

Basic Financial Statements

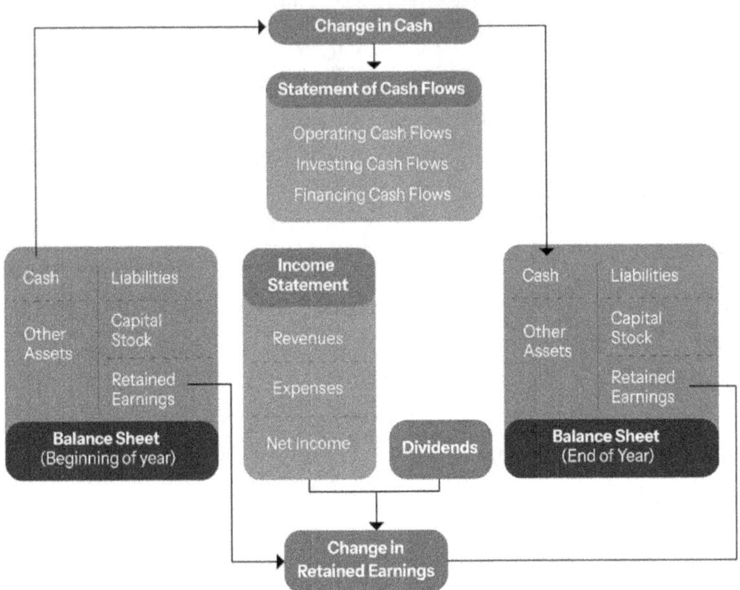

The Three Primary Financial Statements and how they are interconnected in the financial operating system

1. A **Balance Sheet** shows the company's assets, liabilities, and owner's equity, which represent its overall financial health. Changes in assets and liabilities on the balance sheet also influence cash flow. For instance,

purchasing more lumber on credit increases liabilities and assets, affecting future cash on hand without immediately impacting profit.

2. An **Income Statement** tracks revenue and expenses monthly to show profitability. It shows your profit, directly impacting your owner's equity on the balance sheet. Profit increases your business's value (owner's equity); a loss decreases it.

3. **Cash Flow Statements** reveal cash availability—working capital—essential to operations. It complements this by revealing changes in your cash balance. Sometimes, profit may not match cash flows due to non-cash items, such as depreciation or changes in assets and liabilities, which are reflected in the balance sheet.

As illustrated above, these three financial statements are integrated and work together to provide a comprehensive view of your business's financial health, highlighting equity, profitability, cash flow, and overall value. By understanding and connecting these statements, you can make informed decisions to enhance your EBITDA and ensure smooth operations.

* * *

Balance Sheet

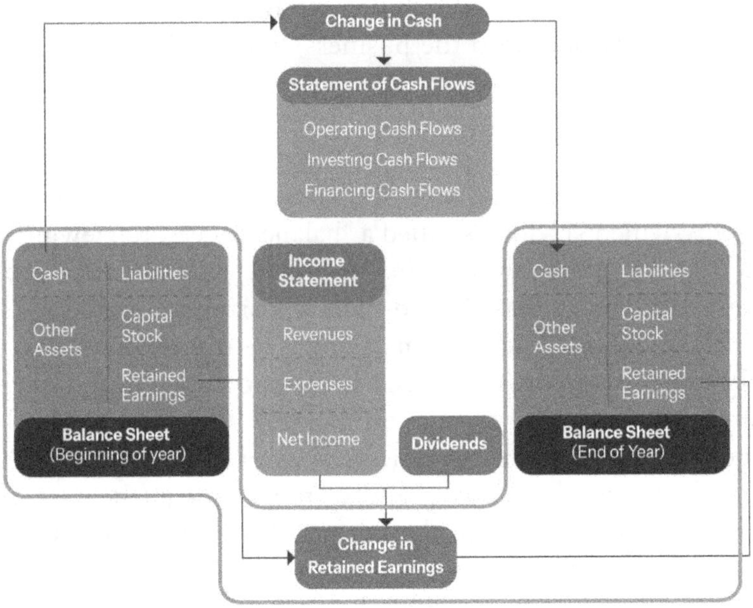

Change in Cash

Statement of Cash Flows

Operating Cash Flows

Investing Cash Flows

Financing Cash Flows

Cash | Liabilities

Other Assets | Capital Stock

Retained Earnings

Balance Sheet
(Beginning of year)

Income Statement

Revenues

Expenses

Net Income

Dividends

Cash | Liabilities

Other Assets | Capital Stock

Retained Earnings

Balance Sheet
(End of Year)

Change in Retained Earnings

The balance sheet is a crucial financial statement that provides a snapshot of a company's financial health at a specific moment in time. The three key components of a balance sheet capture everything the company owns and owes. Note: Each number in the balance sheet categories is listed in order of liquidity.

1. **Assets:** Valuable resources owned by the company that can generate income, including cash, buildings, equipment, inventory, and investments. Think of assets as everything the business owns.

2. **Liabilities:** These are the company's debts or obligations, such as loans, mortgages, accounts payable (money owed to suppliers), and other amounts owed. Liabilities are like the bills the company needs to pay.

3. **Owner's/Shareholder's Equity:** This represents the owner's share of the company's assets after all debts are paid off. It includes retained earnings (profits reinvested into the business) and stock investments. Owner's equity is the owner's claim on the company's assets.

Total assets minus total liabilities always equal owner's equity, which is why it's called a "balance" sheet. Reviewing it at least four times a year helps ensure the company's finances remain balanced and aligned with its performance goals.

The balance sheet is crucial because it provides a snapshot of a company's financial health at a specific point in time, showing how it has performed over the past year. It includes **assets** (valuable items the company owns), **liabilities** (debts or obligations), and **owner's equity** (the portion of assets that belongs to the owner). Additionally, a balance sheet ensures that the total assets equal the sum of liabilities and owners' equity, highlighting the need for a balanced financial state for the company.

As the year draws to a close, Bob decides to review his financial statements to better understand his business's performance and see how he is progressing toward increasing his EBITDA. Among these documents, the balance sheet stands out as a critical tool.

One evening, Bob sat down with his accountant, Sarah, to review the balance sheet. Sarah explains that this document provides a snapshot of his business's financial health at a specific moment in time. It's like a photograph that captures everything the business owns and owes right now.

First, they look at the assets section. Bob sees familiar items like the cash in the business account, his collection of unique live-edge wood slabs, the woodworking tools, and the workshop building. Sarah explains that these are all the things the business owns that have value and can generate income. Assets are organized on the balance sheet in order of their liquidity. Cash is first, followed by cash investments, vehicles, and machinery, and finally, buildings and property.

Next, they move to the liabilities section. Here, Bob notices the loan he took out to purchase high-quality wood, the mortgage on the workshop, and the outstanding payments to his suppliers for raw materials. Sarah points out that these are the debts and obligations the business needs to settle.

Finally, they review the owner's equity. This part shows what remains for Bob after paying off all the business's debts. It includes his initial investment in the business and the profits he has reinvested. Sarah explains that this is Bob's claim on the business's assets. Growing owner's equity shows a healthy reinvestment in the business.

Sarah helps Bob understand that the balance sheet must always be balanced. The total assets should equal the sum of liabilities and owner's equity. It's like a perfectly balanced scale, reflecting the business's financial stability. Net Worth = Assets − Liabilities.

Bob realizes the importance of reviewing the balance sheet at least four times a year. By doing this, he can see how his business has progressed and ensure his finances align with his goals. To improve his EBITDA and grow the company, Bob wants to see positive changes in his year-end balance sheet compared to the start of the year, specifically an increase in owner's equity.

Year-End vs. Start-of-Year Balance Sheet Comparison

Reviewing the balance sheet twice a year—at the beginning and end of the year—can reveal the business's progress.

Sarah and Bob look at the changes in the balance sheet from the start of the year to the end of the year.

1. **Asset Growth**
   - Start of Year: Cash: $50,000, Inventory: $30,000, Equipment: $100,000
   - End of Year: Cash: $70,000, Inventory: $50,000, Equipment: $120,000

Bob sees increases in cash reserves and inventory, along with investments in new equipment and improvements to the workshop.

2. **Liability Management**
   - Start of Year: Accounts Payable: $20,000, Long-term Debt: $80,000
   - End of Year: Accounts Payable: $15,000, Long-term Debt: $75,000

Bob notices a reduction in accounts payable and a manageable level of long-term debt, both of which indicate better cash flow management.

3. **Owner's Equity Increase**
   - Start of Year: Owner's Equity: $80,000
   - End of Year: Owner's Equity: $100,000

Higher retained earnings and overall growth in owner's equity show the business's profitability and reinvestment.

4. **Enhanced Ratios** help refine a more effective interpretation of your financial position.

Improved current and balanced debt-to-equity ratios reflect better financial health and stability. More will be addressed about financial ratios.

Thanks to these positive changes, Bob feels confident that his business is growing and his finances are becoming more robust. This, in turn, contributes to improved EBITDA, allowing Bob to make informed decisions about his company's future.

* * *

Income Statement

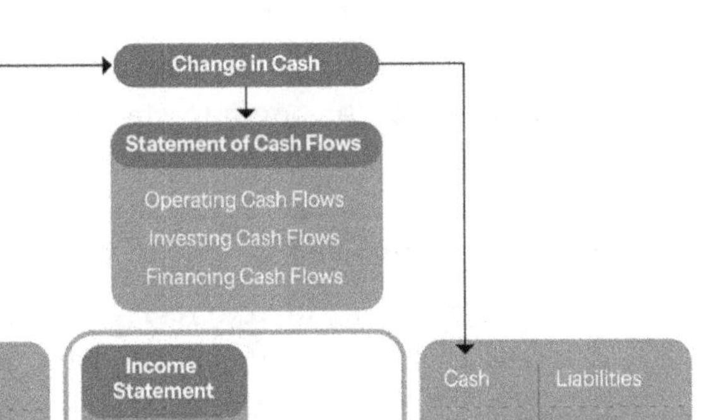

After successfully reviewing his balance sheet, Bob decides to dive into another of the second critical financial documents: the income statement. Also known as a profit and loss statement, it summarizes a company's revenues, expenses, and profits or losses over a specific period. The income statement:

- **Tracks Profitability:** The income statement shows a company's revenues and expenses over a specific period, helping to determine the net profit or loss. This provides a clear picture of the company's profitability.

- **Identifies Revenue Sources and Cost Structures:** It breaks down revenue streams and expenses, allowing businesses to understand which products or services generate the most income and where costs can be reduced or optimized.

- **Aids in Financial Planning and Decision Making:** By analyzing the income statement, businesses can make informed decisions about budgeting, investing, and strategic planning, ensuring that resources are allocated effectively to maximize profitability.

It is recommended to review the Income statement monthly, which requires timely accounting discipline to close out all transactions.

Bob sits down with his accountant, Sarah, to go through the income statement. Sarah explains that the income statement, also known as the profit and loss statement, summarizes revenues, expenses, and profits or losses over a specific period, such as a month, quarter, or year. This helps Bob see how his business has performed during that time frame.

First, they look at the **revenue** section. Bob sees the total income generated from the sale of his unique furniture pieces. This represents the gross sales (total sales before any deductions) and net sales. Bob notes that his gross sales are impressive, showing strong customer demand. After accounting for returns, allowances, and discounts, Bob sees the net sales figure. Sarah explains that net sales provide a more accurate picture of the income Bob's business has retained.

Next, they examine the **Cost of Goods Sold (COGS)**.

- **Raw Materials:** This includes the cost of Bob's beautiful live-edge wood slabs. He notices this cost is significant but necessary for high-quality products.
- **Direct Labor:** The wages paid to skilled craftsmen in Bob's workshop. Bob sees that investing in skilled labor is crucial for maintaining the quality of his furniture.
- **The formula for calculating COGS:** Beginning inventory plus purchases plus direct labor minus ending inventory

Bob then looks at the **gross profit**, calculated by subtracting COGS from net sales. Sarah explains that a healthy gross profit indicates that Bob's business is effectively converting sales into profit before other expenses are accounted for.

They move on to **operating expenses**.

- **Selling Expenses:** These costs are related to marketing and selling the furniture, such as advertising and sales commissions. Bob sees that effective marketing campaigns have helped boost sales.
- **General and Administrative Expenses:** These overhead costs include workshop rent, office salaries, and utilities. Bob understands that controlling these expenses is vital to maintaining profitability.

Next, they review the **operating income**, which is the profit earned from core business operations.

$$\text{Operating Income} = \text{Gross Profit} - \text{Operating Expenses}$$

Sarah notes that a positive operating income shows that Bob's core business activities are profitable.

Bob then examines **other income and expenses**.

- **Interest Income:** Earnings from investments Bob has made. Although small, it contributes positively to the income statement.
- **Interest Expense:** The cost of borrowing money, such as loans used to buy raw materials. Bob sees that managing debt is crucial to keep interest expenses low.
- **Gains or Losses from Sales of Assets:** This includes any profit or loss from the sale of old equipment or assets. Bob notes that careful asset management can affect overall profitability.

Income Before Taxes

They calculate **income before taxes**, which is the total income before income taxes are deducted.

Income Before Taxes = Operating Income +
Other Income - Other Expenses

Sarah explains the **income tax expense**, which includes federal, state, and local taxes that Bob's business must pay. Understanding and planning for taxes helps Bob ensure that he sets aside enough funds to meet tax obligations.

Note: Tax strategy is beyond the scope of this book; however, engaging a good tax accountant can help maximize EBITDA by providing write-off strategies and profitability "timing" decisions.

After deducting all expenses, including taxes, from total revenue, they finally arrive at the **net income**, or total profit.

Net Income = Income Before Taxes -
Income Tax Expense

Bob is pleased to see a healthy net income, indicating that his business is profitable. He realizes that the income statement provides valuable insights into different aspects of his business's financial performance. By carefully reviewing this document, he can make informed decisions to improve profitability and grow the company.

He decides to review the Income Statement monthly to track how initiatives affect the various components of the statement.

A Typical Income Statement Format

Gross Sales	$XXX	
Returns	$XXX	
Discounts	$XXX	
Net Sales	$XXX	Gross Sales - Returns - Discounts
Cost of Goods Sold	$XXX	
Gross Profit	$XXX	Net Sales - Cost of Goods Sold
Operating Expenses		
Selling Expenses	$XXX	
General and Administrative	$XXX	
Total Operating Expenses	$XXX	Selling Expenses + General and Adminstrative Expenses
Operating Income	$XXX	Gross Profit - Total Operating Expenses
Other Income and Expenses		
Interest Income	$XXX	
Interest Expense	($XXX)	
Gain/Loss on Sale of Assets	$XXX	
Total Other Income/Expense	$XXX	Interest Income - Interest Expense +/- Gain/Loss on Sale of Assets
Income Before Taxes	$XXX	
Income Tax Expense	$XXX	
Net Income	**$XXX**	Income Before Taxes - Income Tax Expense

* * *

Cash Flow Statement

As we mentioned earlier, a cash flow statement is a crucial financial document that tracks cash inflows and outflows, highlighting cash generated from daily operations, investments in assets, and financing activities. It is divided into three sections.

- **Operating Activities:** This section details the cash generated or used in the company's daily operations, including cash received from customers and cash paid to suppliers and employees. It provides insight into the money flowing in and out of regular business activities.

- **Investing Activities:** This part focuses on cash flows from investments in assets such as property, equipment, and interest-bearing financial investments. It includes cash spent on asset purchases and cash received from asset sales, highlighting the company's investments to support growth.

- **Financing Activities:** This section outlines cash flow related to financing the company's operations, such as issuing or repurchasing stock, paying dividends, and managing loans. It shows the money moving in and out from investors and lenders to fund the company's financial needs.

The cash flow statement is like a diary of a company's cash movements. It tells us where the money is coming from and where it's going. By understanding how cash flows in and out of the company, we can gauge its ability to meet its financial obligations, invest in growth, and reward shareholders. Reviewing cash positions weekly is highly recommended. Cash is King.

The Cash Flow Statement: A Diary of Financial Movements

By understanding his cash flow statement, Bob can gauge his company's liquidity, ensure bills are paid on time, and plan for future growth. First, Bob and Sarah look at the operating activities section. Sarah explains that this section is like tracking the money coming in and going out from running the business. For example, Bob sees that cash inflows from customers are healthy, indicating strong sales of his unique furniture pieces. However, he also notices significant cash outflows to suppliers for raw materials and payments to his skilled craftsmen. By managing these daily cash flows, Bob can ensure his business operations run smoothly.

Next, they examine the investing activities section. Sarah likens it to the money spent on buying new stuff or making investments to help the business grow. Bob notices that he has spent a considerable amount on new woodworking equipment to improve production efficiency. While this investment reduces cash in the short term, it is expected to boost productivity and profitability in the long run. He also sees some cash inflows from selling older equipment, offsetting some of the new investment costs. Always buy assets that deliver strong returns on investment and positive cash flow.

Finally, they review the financing activities section. Sarah explains that this section is like the money coming in or going out from sources like investors or lenders to support the company's financial needs. Bob observes that his company recently took out a loan to finance a major expansion project. This loan appears as a cash inflow in the financing activities section. He also sees cash outflows for loan repayments and dividend payments to shareholders, reflecting the company's commitment to financial obligations and rewarding its investors.

The Importance of the Cash Flow Statement

Many companies ignore the cash flow statement because they are so intent on profit. However, the cash flow statement shows how much money is in the bank right now—the money needed to pay bills like electricity, cell phones, vendor invoices, and payroll.

Sarah shares a cautionary tale.

I once worked with a retail client who sold arts and crafts supplies. She hired an email marketing company to grow her email list and boost sales.

The marketing company provided a contract specifying their duties, weekly email count, and reporting methods. A 30-day notice made it simple for her to terminate the contract. Once the client signed, the email marketing company started.

Their weekly emails boosted her sales by offering new deals, attracting more orders, and improving revenue per order. In short, they made the client money. Despite regular communication, the client was silent.

Their work continued as stipulated in the contract, which made no mention of ceasing work upon non-approval. One day, after the monthly fee was charged, the client called, furious, claiming the marketing company had no right to charge her and that they were draining their cash balance and taking funds allocated for payroll.

She argued that her lack of approval of weekly offers and emails absolved her of any debt to the company. She filed a chargeback. The chargeback was reversed, and the email marketing company got its money. We never learned what happened to her payroll.

The moral of the story? She hadn't been paying attention to her cash flow statement, which indicates her available funds for paying bills, in this case, critical payroll funds.

This story highlights the importance of regularly reviewing the cash flow statement to avoid financial mismanagement and ensure sufficient funds are available to cover essential expenses.

Bob realizes the value of the cash flow statement in managing his business effectively. By regularly monitoring his cash flow, he can make informed decisions, avoid financial pitfalls, and ensure his company remains healthy and poised for growth.

Consider using cash management sweep accounts to optimize cash. Proactively leverage cash flow timing by collecting accounts receivable sooner than accounts payable and paying vendors with the cash inflow from customers. Then consider sweeping the excess cash into a debt-reduction or self-funded asset-procurement account. Make it a regular practice to monitor "automatic" expense renewals to ensure continued value is being added.

Enhanced Ratios

We will now delve deeper into the Enhanced Ratios to use to create your EBITDA Key Performance Indicator Report Card. Once you understand your financial statements, the next step is to **interpret your performance in context**. Financial ratios transform raw numbers into actionable insights, and the most widely accepted benchmarks for this purpose are the **Robert Morris Ratios**, published by the **Risk Management Association (RMA)**.

RMA collects data from thousands of privately held companies across hundreds of industries and organizes the results by **industry code** and company size. The annual statement studies provide **median, upper-quartile**, and **lower-quartile** ratios, allowing you to see exactly how your business stacks up against industry peers.

The ratios are grouped into five key categories:

- **Liquidity**—ability to meet short-term obligations
- **Activity (turnover)**---operational efficiency
- **Leverage**—use of debt vs. equity
- **Profitability**—margins and returns
- **Coverage**—debt service capacity

By comparing your ratios to RMA benchmarks, you can quickly identify strengths, weaknesses, and opportunities. For example, a **low current ratio** may signal liquidity concerns, while a **high inventory turnover** relative to peers may reveal operational advantages. Banks and buyers rely on these benchmarks to assess financial health—so should you.

Integrating ratio analysis into your annual planning gives you a clear, objective view of performance.

The Cash Flow to Debt Ratio and the Cash Return on Equity Ratio are the first to consider because they are derived from the cash flow statement and the balance sheet. They are part of further financial analysis to get a more accurate read of your financial position.

1. **Cash Flow to Debt Ratio**
   - *Definition:* The **Cash Flow to Debt Ratio** measures a company's ability to repay its total debt (both short-term and long-term) using cash generated from its core operations. It shows how many times a company's annual operating cash flow can cover its total debt obligations.
   - *Formula:* Cash Flow to Debt Ratio = Operating Cash Flow / Total Debt
   - *Interpretation:* A **Higher Ratio** means there is a stronger ability to repay debt from operations and less reliance on external financing. A **Lower Ratio** indicates higher leverage risk, which could indicate insufficient operational cash flow to service debt.
     - For example, if Bob's business has $1,200,000 in Operating Cash Flow and $4,000,000 in total debt, the **Cash Flow to Debt** would be 30 percent. This means Bob's business's cash flow covers 30 percent of the total debt.

2. **Cash Return on Equity Ratio**
   - *Definition:* The **Cash Return on Equity (CROE)** measures how effectively a company generates cash from its shareholders' equity. Unlike the traditional Return on Equity (ROE), which uses net income,

CROE uses **operating cash flow**, making it a more conservative, liquidity-focused measure of shareholder returns.

- ○ *Formula:* Cash Return on Equity = Operating Cash Flow / Average Shareholders' Equity
- ○ *Interpretation:* A **Higher CROE** means the company is generating strong cash flow relative to the equity invested by shareholders. **Lower CROE** indicates weaker cash-generating efficiency from shareholders' capital. **Advantage over Return On Equity:** Removes accounting distortions from accruals and non-cash items, focusing purely on cash performance.

  - For example, if Bob's business has $200,000 in Operating Cash Flow and $1,000,000 in Average Shareholders' Equity, the Cash Return on Equity would be 20 percent. This means for every dollar Bob has invested in this company, here's how much **real cash** the business is generating from its operations. A 20 percent return is not a bad start.

Identifying the most critical ratios aligned with your priority goals to leverage a clear, customized understanding of your progress is suggested. The following is a representative list of the most relevant financial ratios to consider for further analysis.

Master List of Financial Ratios

Profitability Ratios

Net Proft on Net Sales	Net Proft / Net Sales
Net Profit on Tangible Net Worth	Net Profit / Tangible Net Worth
Net Profit on Total Assets	Net Profit / Total Assets
Gross Profit on Net Sales	Gross Profit / Net Sales

Efficiency Ratios

Net Sales to Total Assets	Annual Net Sales / Total Assets
Net Sales to Net Working Capital	Annual Net Sales Net / Working Capital
Inventory to Net Working Capital	Inventory Cost Net / Working Capital
Collection Period	(Accounts Recievable / Annual Net Credit Sales) x 360
Excess Funds in Receivables	Excess Days Beyond Median x (Annual Net Credits Sales / 360)
Net Sales to Inventory	Annual Net Sales / Inventory Cost
Excess Funds in Inventory	Inventory Cost - (Annual Net Sales Median Inventory Turnover)
Accounts Payable to Net Sales	Annual Net Sales / Inventory Cost
Short Term Loans Turnover	(Short Term Loans Annual Purchases) x 360

Solvency Ratios

Current Assets to Current Debt	Current Assets / Current Debt
Liquid Assets to Current Debt	Current Assets - (Inventory and Prepaid Expenses)
Fixed Assets to Tangible Networth	Net Fixed Assets / Tangible Networth *Net Fixed Assets = Fixed Assets After Depreciation*
Excess Funds in Fixed Assets	Fixed Assets (After Depreciation) - Average Investment in Fixed Assets *Average Investment in Fixed Assets = Tangible Networth x Median Fixed Assets)*
Curret Debt to Tangible Net Worth	Current Liabilies / Tangible Net Worth
Total Debt to Tangible Net Worth	Total Liabilities / Tangible Net Worth
Long-term Debt Payback	Net Profits Current Year Depreciation *Current portion of long-term debt principle only, not interest)*
Accounts Payable Turnover	(Accounts Payable Annual Purchases) x 360

CHAPTER 10

Lever 5: Profit Process Formula

In business, feedback is the breakfast of champions.
—Ken Blanchard

It's time to evaluate every business procedure in order to develop your Profit Process Formula. Brace yourself; this could hurt a bit.

We're examining every system in the company, no matter how small or intricate. Instead of a series of departmental silos, picture your business as a relay race—departments smoothly and efficiently passing the baton. This is rather understandable from a broad perspective. That's how you'd ideally run your business.

However, when an owner spends most of their time working **in** the business—handling daily tasks—instead of working **on** the business through strategic development, they risk creating silos and missing key opportunities. It's easy for both leaders and employees to forget that a business operates like a living body: for it to move and thrive, every part must function in harmony. Likewise, for a business to perform profitably and operate at its peak, all departments and processes must work together seamlessly, pursuing the goal to reach perpetual prime.

The Profit Process Formula accounts for every facet of the business to ensure there are resources, assets, systems, and processes in place to efficiently fulfill customer demands, get paid in a timely manner, and identify bottlenecks. A process bottleneck is a point in a system where the flow of tasks or materials is constrained by limited capacity, slowing down the overall output and efficiency of the entire process. Just like a narrow bottleneck in a physical bottle restricts the speed of the liquid flowing through it, these bottlenecks in work processes create a point of congestion, leading to delays, backlogs, and reduced productivity.

Once you establish what's happening now, you can determine what needs to happen to improve the cycle. This is your Profit Process Formula. An important aspect of this is engaging your key players. They will become more important as you move into a strategic position.

Bob is at his desk, flowcharting the business the old school way on paper and pencil, when Jamie comes in with coffee.

"Here you go, Boss," he says. "What'cha doing?"

"That's a good question. Actually, you can help me," he said. "I'm trying to flow chart the business to see where we can improve things, but I'm a bit blind." He hands him the flow chart. "Can you take a look and let me know what I'm missing?"

Jamie was the perfect one to help. He started working on the warehouse floor with inventory before moving into production. From there, he moved up to orders, marketing, and finally, sales before working as Bob's assistant. He has always focused on building relationships with people in other departments. He has firsthand knowledge of the overall process flow.

"Bob, this is a good start. The first thing I see is that you're addressing the big ideas—like advertising—without delving into the distinction between advertising and marketing. Do you mind if I take this for a few days? I'd like to talk with a few people, if that's okay with you." Jamie said.

"Of course. Thanks for taking this on, Jamie."

Several days later, Jamie scheduled two hours on Bob's calendar.

"Hi Jamie, two hours? What's going on that we need two hours on a Friday?" Bob asked.

"I finished your flow chart," Jamie said. "It's as complete as I can make it, which means it's really detailed. We'll need the full two hours to go over it."

The Profit Process Formula examines every stage of acquiring business, from qualifying and selecting prospects to converting them into customers. Then, we consider the various ways customers interact with our system: phone, fax, email, direct sales, email campaigns, sales teams, and trade shows. Next, we assess the demand and present a proposal to customers, involving internal procedures to ensure you understand your expenses and profits. This way, you can be confident that any proposal made will be profitable for you.

Following the quote, the customer submits a purchase order that details the terms, conditions, and expectations for their procurement. An order acknowledgement confirms order details and addresses any discrepancies in requests, demands, or lead times with the customer. The order becomes a work order, and then operations schedules it. Purchasing then is informed of purchasing requirements and orders the required goods and services.

You then obtain the needed products or produce them using your inventory and resources, schedule asset use, and complete the finished product. Once finished, it's packaged, labeled, and prepared for shipping. Next, establish the freight quote and terms; then, ship the product and follow up to ensure it meets the customer's needs.

Following that, you'll begin collecting payments and following up to ensure everything is paid in full. Upon receiving payment, your systems will be updated to reflect it, and the funds will be sent to the bank. We use it to track cash flow, sales income, and profitability. Examining the complex profit process system that covers all organizational processes reveals significant EBITDA growth opportunities.

This overall process is to be graphically laid out in detail to identify every facet of the profit relay race. The following is a very high-level graph of a typical flow of business activity. In reality, delving into the flow chart details of each subprocess is where true EBITDA growth is identified.

CLOSED LOOP: MANAGING THE VALUE CHAIN

Continuously refine the profit formula for efficiency and effectiveness.

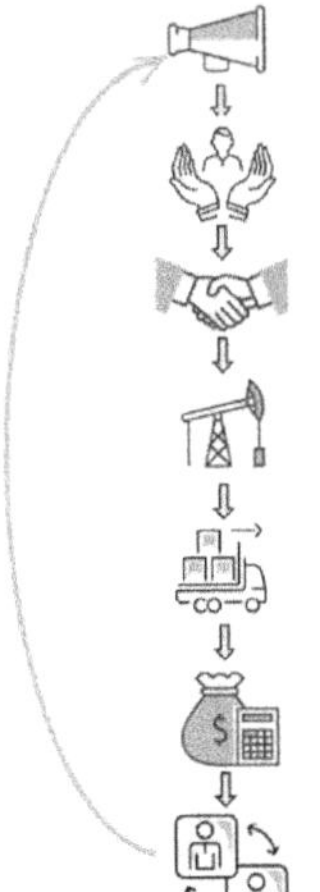

Inputs: marketing, advertising, established accounts

Prospecting: customer acquisition

Establish Account: customer signs contract

Production: convert raw materials to finished goods

Distribution: ship products

Invoicing: get paid

Post Sale Survey: acquire feedback from customers

What does your detailed profit process look like?

CHAPTER 11

Lever 6:
Sales and Psychographics

Stop selling. Start helping.
—Zig Ziglar

You're ready. It's time to increase sales. I caution you. There is no quick answer or easy step to increase your sales. That's the way it should be. We're building a foundation for long-term growth, not a quick cash infusion.

It's time to settle in. This is a hefty section. Sales growth depends on understanding psychographics, market share, marketing, sales processes, customer retention, and the competition. We will begin by examining psychographics, as this forms the foundation of understanding your customer—their desires and motivations.

Psychographics

In today's marketplace, understanding *who* your customer is no longer provides a competitive edge—you must understand *why* they buy, *how* they think, and *what* truly drives their decisions. That's where **psychographics** come in. Psychographics go beyond surface-level demographics like age, income, and geography, delving into the psychology of your audience—their values, beliefs, attitudes, motivations, and lifestyles. This chapter explores how uncovering these inner drivers can transform your approach to marketing, sales, and product design. By understanding what your customers care about most, you can connect with them not just logically, but emotionally—creating stronger brands, more loyal customers, and ultimately, more profitable businesses.

Psychographics outline the specific characteristics and needs of your customers and prospects. It answers the question:

- Who is your customer?
- How do the customers differ from one another (ex., how the smallest customer differs from the largest customer)?
- What is the customer buying?
- Why are they buying it?
- What is the product's significance in improving their customers' businesses?

Psychographic analysis reveals the key elements influencing customer purchasing decisions. This includes their company size, industry, cultural aspects (such as virtues, values, and missions), and the factors that drive their supplier selection. This analysis enables the company to craft more effective marketing that aligns with customer expectations.

Although these systems offer advanced psychological analysis, applying psychographics effectively requires common sense. Psychographics clarify the emotions your product fulfills and the features and capabilities buyers desire. Psychographics, therefore, shouldn't be overlooked.

Bob grew by meeting customer demand. It wasn't planned; it just happened. His growth was a reaction. His system held a vast number of Stock Keeping Units (SKUs) because each product was custom-designed. While customers were very satisfied with the wide selection, Bob found scheduling increasingly difficult due to the unique nature of each task.

By analyzing current and potential client needs, Bob identified areas for improvement. Based on this marketing data, Bob altered his production methods. He began creating products using common components, rather than custom-made ones, while also focusing on efficient manufacturing. Bob realized that his customers love how his products look and feel, but they do not need custom pieces each time.

Identifying common components across his product range helped Bob improve production efficiency and save money by standardizing the bill of materials. He called this a product standardization initiative. The whole thing came about thanks to Bob's grasp of his customers' psychological profiles.

Bob's experience leads us into market share, which is the percentage of customers in your industry that you hold. It's vital to analyze your industry, customer base, and potential customer base. Accurately determining market share is often a challenge. However, establishing a fundamental metric enables companies to evaluate their growth in any industry.

Measuring market share involves identifying your customers' industries, organized by Standard Industrial Classification (SIC) code, then counting your customers and prospects within that industry. Your market share is simply the number of your customers in that SIC code divided by the total number of potential customers in that SIC code. You possess a basic yet highly effective method for calculating initial market share.

A more advanced approach could involve assessing total market capitalization by ranking prospects by sales and determining the percentage of their spending on your offerings. This reveals the market's growth potential and your sales opportunities. We'll use the basic number of customers divided by the potential customers approach because it will provide a valuable, cost-effective metric for tracking market share.

Once you have your market share, define your sales process. It is extremely critical to establish a clear, concise process for pursuing potential customers and to continue refining it as you grow.

We begin by evaluating. Using your Customer Relationship Management (CRM) software, categorize your current customers by their SIC code. Instead of your sales-by-customer report, generate one showing sales by industry. This clarifies your earnings in a particular industry.

Prioritize your markets, starting with the top and working down. Plan to specify and define all the market needs and pinpoint the required details. This helps you identify potential clients who share similar measurable characteristics with your best clients, creating a targeted list for future outreach. For example, you realize you have a large concentration of business in a particular industry in a specific geographic regional cluster. The aim is to identify prospects in the same industry located in other high-concentration regions.

Once you understand what your potential customers need, identifying your target audience becomes simpler. Determine the optimal outreach strategies (e.g., direct sales, email marketing, trade shows) and identify the key decision-makers within each organization.

Realize that your customers' purchasing, aka key decision-makers, is sometimes handled by sales professionals, other times by procurement professionals. Sometimes it's the CEO, sometimes it's the COO. Determining who makes procurement decisions is vital. Analyzing your CRM database identifies high-value prospects.

To create a strong value proposition, you should consider potential customers' psychographics, market demand,

and your organization's perceived value. Saving customers money and improving purchase quality through consistent supply is a succinct value proposition example. This enhances your brand and company. It's strategically designed to meet your demands, ensuring that there are no stockouts.

The following graphic is a value proposition chart to help create effective value propositions and deliver them with persuasive conviction. This will certainly help build trust and rapport with the key decision makers for your customers and prospects.

Value Proposition and Units of Conviction Chart

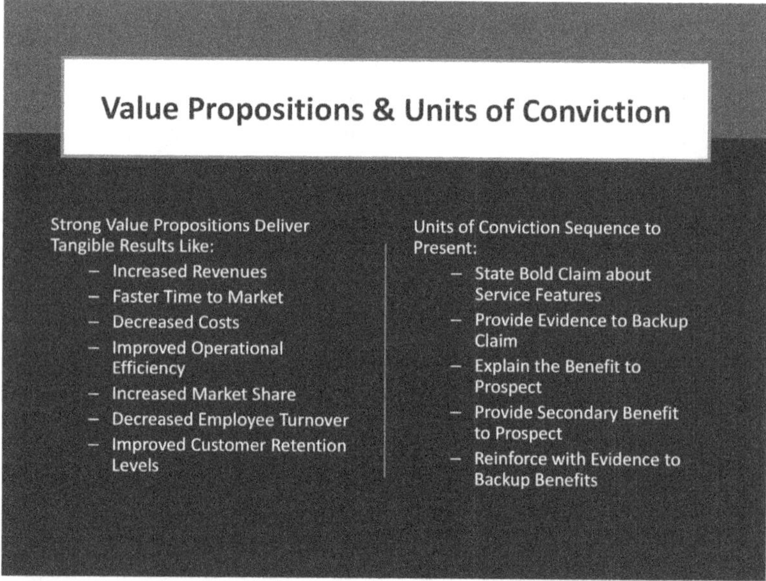

After identifying prospective customers by analyzing and emulating your best clients' shared characteristics, aligning them with your value proposition, and applying your key **units of conviction** (the measurable proofs of your value), it's time to engage. Reach out consistently and purposefully.

The goal is to convert prospects into customers by earning a bid request and ultimately closing the deal. Remember, this process rarely succeeds on the first try. Each attempt provides valuable feedback—insights that should refine your message, improve your approach, and strengthen your connection. Winning in business requires persistence and adaptability; **continuous effort, combined with continuous improvement**, ultimately turns prospects into loyal customers.

Customer retention is key; thus, all internal processes must prioritize customer satisfaction to encourage repeat business. Exceeding customer expectations should be a primary goal. At a minimum, meet expectations without any errors or flaws. Errors and flaws do occur. Swift, efficient resolution of these problems is critical, as it significantly enhances the relationship and fosters goodwill. Problem-solving skills are highly valued and a strong indicator of quality in services or products. Effectively solving problems is a key distinguishing factor in building a solid customer support team.

Finally, understanding the customer analysis process and customer acquisition costs is crucial. The next step is to determine your customers' lifetime value (CLTV) based on their acquisition cost, generated revenue, and profit, as well as the length of your business relationship with them. Recognize that they represent a valuable investment in your company, whose long-term customer relationships are a source of pride and growing EBITDA. Know your customers' lifetime value.

Marketing

Now that you know your potential customers, you can start marketing to them. Marketing is a vast field, with entire books and companies dedicated to its intricacies. While we won't delve into all its complexities here, it's crucial to establish a strong foundation in marketing fundamentals to set up your EBITDA integration strategy effectively.

Bob sits back for a moment. Reviewing his EBITDA integration strategy, he recalls his ambitious goal of doubling revenue to $10 million, a crucial step toward doubling EBITDA.

He's been focused on improving the internal functions of the business. Now it's time to look outward at the company's sales.

Before you can sell a product, you need to introduce it to the marketplace and build awareness. That is where marketing comes in. First, you'll note that I said "marketing" rather than "advertising." Advertising is a method. Marketing is a strategy.

There are many factors to consider. For now, we're going to look at four factors in developing your marketing strategy.

- **Product Quality:** He crafts beautiful, functional art pieces from the highest quality live-edge wood, including tables, dressers, chairs, and bed frames.

- **Emotional Appeal:** His pieces evoke feelings of sophistication, a connection with nature, and peace.

- **Pricing Strategy:** His products range from $400 for the smallest pieces to over $10,000 for the largest, with an average order value of $3,250.

- **Customer Base:** His clientele includes mid- to high-net-worth individuals, institutions, and businesses, whom he reaches through luxury home magazines and his internal sales team. He recognizes the need to invest in an outside sales team but is often sidetracked by day-to-day tasks.

Bob runs the company's top-line numbers.

➤ *Current Annual Revenue:* $5,300,000
➤ *Average Order Value:* $3,250
➤ *Annual Orders:* 1,631

➢ *Revenue Goal:* $10 million
➢ *Required Orders:* At $3,250 per order, achieving this goal requires 3,077 orders per year, representing a 1,446-order increase annually or 121 new orders per month.
➢ Note that it is critical to account for annual business attrition; therefore, making up lost business is just the new starting point for growing sales.

The challenge lies in attracting the additional 1,446 orders through a mix of current and new customers, adding to fill in for any attrition / lost business that occurs.

Bob examines his current customer demographics by category.

- ❖ **Customer Types**
  - ➢ Mid- to high-net-worth individuals
  - ➢ Institutions
  - ➢ Businesses
- ❖ **Order Frequency**
  - ➢ Individuals place approximately 1,500 orders per year.
  - ➢ Institutions place about 45 orders annually.
  - ➢ Businesses place around 85 orders each year.
- ❖ **Order Value by Customer Type**
  - ➢ Individuals: $2,750 per order
  - ➢ Institutions: $10,380 per order
  - ➢ Businesses: $8,150 per order

To generate the additional $4,700,000 in revenue, Bob identifies three key components of a marketing campaign: who, what, and how.

- **Who:** Identifying the target customers.
- **What:** Determining what they are purchasing.
- **How:** Strategizing on the best methods to reach them.

Bob considers various marketing approaches, whether focusing on individuals, institutions, businesses, or a combination of these. Realizing the need for a data-driven strategy, he tasks his sales team with analyzing their Customer Relationship Management (CRM) system to develop a solid plan.

The Company's CRM system is designed to help them:

- Define markets
- Measure market share
- Identify decision-making units, the position that makes buying decisions
- Identify their pain points and demographic information
- Target them with value-delivering solutions tied to your brand and products as solutions
- Know the lifetime value of a customer
- Understand annual attrition rates

Building a CRM System

Establishing and maintaining strong customer relationships is essential for business growth, and a CRM tool is crucial for achieving this. Businesses, whether small or large, benefit from implementing CRM systems to organize customer data and enhance relationship management.

Effective CRM systems include critical fields such as customer details, industry codes, contact information, and transaction history. Analyzing this data allows businesses to identify their best and worst customers, understand customer demographics, and tailor marketing strategies accordingly.

Essential CRM Fields

- **Customer Details:** Name, industry SIC code, type (residential, commercial, small business, large business, etc.), address (street, city, state, zip code), website, email, phone number, contact name(s)

- **Financial Information:** Annual spend with the company, customer total revenue, payment behavior (early, on-time, or late)

- **Customer Insights:** Notes, employee treatment (how they treat your employees), contact details, birthdays, etc.

- **Recency, Frequency, Monetary (RFM):** RFM is a customer segmentation technique used in marketing to evaluate and rank customers based on their purchase behavior. It helps businesses identify and target their most valuable customers based on their historical buying patterns.

- **Customer Lifetime Value (CLV):** A metric that measures the total revenue a business can earn from a customer during the lifetime of their relationship. It helps optimize marketing, prioritize retention, and focus on high-value customers to maximize long-term profitability. CLV guides decisions on customer acquisition versus retention. It helps optimize marketing spending and ROI. It supports a strategic focus on high-value customers to achieve long-term profitability.

These fields help businesses build detailed customer profiles, enabling better customer segmentation, targeted marketing, and stronger customer relationships.

Analyzing Your CRM

Building and Utilizing Prospect Lists

Creating a comprehensive prospect list based on ideal client profiles and industry classifications is a critical step in leveraging your CRM. Understanding the CLV enables businesses to make informed decisions about customer acquisition and retention strategies, ultimately driving profitability and sustainable growth.

Engaging Your Team for CRM Analysis

Utilize and lead your team's intellect and expertise to analyze the CRM. This process requires time to explore and define several key aspects:

- **Identifying Best and Worst Customers:** Determine your best and worst customers and understand the reasons behind these classifications.

- **Industries Served:** Catalog the different industries your customers belong to, helping to identify which sectors are most lucrative and where there may be growth opportunities.

- **Customer Types:** Assess whether you serve individuals, institutions, residential, commercial, or business customers—small or large, specific demographics, or a mix of these.

- **Customer Demographics:** Analyze your customer base's demographics, including age and gender segments (e.g., women aged 25–40 vs. men aged 30–50).

- **Average Customer Value:** Calculate the average value of your customers.

- **Top Spender Analysis:** Identify the top spender from the previous year and understand acquisition channels, marketing strategies, or referral sources that led them to your business.

- **Lowest Spender Analysis:** Identify the lowest spender from the previous year and understand the acquisition process to identify the gaps or inefficiencies.

- **Creating Customer Profiles:** Develop detailed profiles for different customer types to better target and serve each segment. Develop avatar-like representations of markets and customer profiles to identify and target prospects.

- **Analyze Geographic Concentration Factors:** Analyze geographic locations, cluster them by sales representation, and identify cultural nuances to blend in and represent with a local flair.

The Customer Lifetime Value should be a major component of the marketing strategy. Evaluate the long-term value of customers by analyzing their acquisition costs, spending patterns, and retention rates. Examine which marketing channels generated the highest-value orders. Use this information to focus on high-value customers and develop targeted strategies to enhance customer loyalty and increase lifetime value.

This in-depth analysis enables businesses to tailor their marketing efforts, strengthen customer relationships, and refine their overall business strategy.

Marketing Strategy: The Who, What, and How

While CRM data helps you understand who your target customers are, effective marketing also requires understanding what they are purchasing and how to reach them.

- **Who:** Identifying the target customers through detailed CRM analysis, focusing on demographics, customer types, and industries served.
- **What:**
  - Determining the core emotion the purchase solves: time, money, image, love, vanity, fear, and intricacies thereof.
  - Determining what products or services solve the problems these customers have.
  - Determining purchase frequency, analyzing sales data to identify trends, and identifying high-demand offerings.
  - Determining the most effective value propositions customers react to.
- **How:** Strategizing the best methods to reach these customers by leveraging insights from acquisition channels, marketing strategies, customer journey mapping, and engagement tactics. This might include online advertising, social media campaigns, personalized email marketing, direct sales approaches, or leveraging referral networks.

Integrating these elements ensures a comprehensive marketing strategy that not only identifies and understands your target customers but also effectively engages and retains them, driving long-term business growth.

Use customer demographics to identify prospects by extrapolating key criteria and searching for companies with characteristics similar to your best customers. You can get a strong understanding of your prospects by understanding your customers.

Branding

Branding is *not* about selling, but about activating emotions and enhancing brand awareness. Branding is your competitive edge. There is growing evidence that having a powerful brand is a critical component of business success. A 2012 McKinsey & Co. study found that strong brands outperformed weak brands by 20 percent, and typically outperformed the market.[3]

In the simplest terms, a brand is what the organization stands for and the unifying theme of the company—the reason the business exists. Ideally, it is a simple concept that is both distinctive and memorable for internal and external audiences. A brand encompasses the business's value proposition and competitive advantage in the marketplace.

Famous brands include:

❖ Coca-Cola®: joy, sharing, refreshment

---

[3] "Business Branding," McKinsey & Company, March 2013, https://www.mckinsey.com/~/media/McKinsey/Business Functions/Marketing and Sales/Our Insights/B2B Business branding/1-McKinsey-Business-Branding-Bringing-Strategy-to-Life_0.pdf.

- ❖ Apple®: simplicity, exclusivity, innovation, design, premium quality
- ❖ Kellogg's®: childhood, nostalgia, simple and healthy lifestyle
- ❖ Subaru®: love, adventure, safety, cost-efficient

Many retailers and customers purchased Bob's products and resold them. Bob gained a strong reputation with these retailers. Retailers expanded their brand by purchasing, rebranding, and significantly increasing the price of Bob's products, which enhanced their market image. Bob sold this retail segment a private label product.

Bob was happy for a time, but the desire to build his own brand led him to worry about competing with his loyal customers. After careful consideration, Bob developed a strong brand strategy that embodied his values, company strengths, and value propositions, revitalizing his existing brand to better reflect his vision. It was a huge success. Establishing his identity with customers took considerable time, as other customers had already established their brands with his products. His established brand continued to thrive, retaining his original customer base while expanding his "new" brand and growing his private-label sales to other retailers.

Proactive, strong branding improves your company's market visibility and boosts sales. Aligning a clear direction with the company's mission enhances operational efficiency and EBITDA growth.

There are entire books, companies, and online courses devoted to branding. For this book and to improve your EBITDA, we'll focus on a few key questions to help you think about what your brand is now and what you want it to be.

Identifying and Implementing Brands

Before you can rebuild your brand, you need to understand your current brand. If you're unsure about your current brand, follow these steps to identify and understand it.

1. **Internal Reflection**
   - *Core Values:* Reflect on the core values that drive your business decisions and practices. What principles are non-negotiable for your company?
   - *Mission and Vision:* Revisit your company's mission and vision statements. What is your purpose, and what long-term goals are you striving to achieve?

2. **Conduct a Brand Workshop with Employees**
   - Gather key stakeholders—leadership, marketing, and customer service—to discuss and brainstorm your brand identity.
   - Facilitate activities that help articulate the company's values, mission, and vision.

3. **Talk with Customers**
   - *Customer Interviews and Surveys:* Engage directly with your customers through interviews and surveys to gather their perceptions of your brand. Ask them what they think your company stands for, what they value most about your products or services, and how they would describe their experiences with your brand.
   - *Focus Groups:* Organize sessions with a diverse group of customers to gain deeper insights into their views and feelings about your brand. Use these sessions to explore common themes and areas for improvement.

- o *Feedback Analysis:* Review existing customer feedback, such as online reviews, social media comments, and customer service interactions. Look for patterns in how customers describe your brand and what aspects they highlight.

4. **Engage a Brand Consultant**
   - o Consider hiring a branding expert or consultant who can provide an objective assessment of your current brand and guide you through the process.

5. **Analyze Data and Insights**
   - o Use data from customer surveys, market research, and internal feedback to identify patterns and themes that can inform your brand identity. Look for commonalities in how your company is perceived.

6. **Create Brand Personas**
   - o Develop detailed profiles of your ideal customers, including their needs, preferences, and behaviors. Use these personas to align your brand with your target audience's expectations and desires.

7. **Test and Refine**
   - o Develop initial concepts for your brand identity and test them with small focus groups or through pilot campaigns to refine them. Gather feedback and refine your brand elements based on the responses you receive. Recency, Frequency, and Monetary (RFM) data will provide very lucrative insights.

By following these steps, you can gain a clearer understanding of your current brand and take actionable steps to define and strengthen it, ensuring it aligns with your business goals. You can also begin redefining it to better reflect who you want to be and resonate with your audience.

Understanding and defining your brand is crucial for business success, as it shapes customer perception and drives competitive advantage. By thoroughly analyzing internal and external insights, businesses can craft a consistent and compelling brand identity that resonates with their target audience and supports long-term growth. Make sure your brand resonates with your company culture and the team's competencies. Do not try to be someone you are not. Be authentic.

Competition

Know your competition, be familiar with them, but do not obsess about them. Become deeply invested in and obsessed with your customers and prospects instead. It is a better return on your entrepreneurial efforts.

Competition can be intimidating. You're in good company; even seasoned business leaders feel the same. But here's some advice: ignore the competition. That's right. Ignore them.

Initially, I advised you to build your EBITDA integration strategy with a competitive analysis. Now, I want you to have the experience of ripping it up and throwing it out like junk mail.

"But I need to know what they're doing. I need to know if they're stealing my customers. I need to know what products they're selling so I can mimic them. I need to know… I need to know…"

Go ahead, continue that thought. How much do you need to know? How much is enough? You've studied your competition. You may have extensive knowledge about them, including their marketing strategy, product lines, and top customers. But let's try something new: focus less on them. In fact, take the time you spend thinking about competition and transfer 99 percent of that time, energy, and effort to concentrate on your customers and prospects. This will generate a far greater return.

Reacting constantly to what competitors are doing and how they're doing it keeps you on the defensive. If you still want to keep an eye on them, do it smartly. List the main competitors, noting one strength and one weakness for each. But your main goal? Building up your own business so that it becomes tough for others to match. Focus all your attention on your customers and prospects and let the competition obsess about YOUR company. Rather, think about how to build barriers to protect your business from the competition.

Possible competitor barriers to market entry to building your EBITDA are:

- Trademarks
- Patents
- Trade Secrets
- Proprietary designs
- Exclusive knowledge
- Customized software programs
- Customized, documented engineering processes
- Documented training systems
- Proprietary databases
- Published articles or industry press
- Licenses and permits
- Crucial contracts
- Exceptional customer service

Instead of being obsessed with competitors, become obsessed with your customers, prospects, and the features and benefits of your products and services that will enamor them.

Next, let's talk about establishing a real connection with your customers. It is you, the owner, who should initially have conversations with them. Here are some things you might consider asking them directly:

- How's your business?

- What problems are you having?

- Is there any way we can assist you?

- Describe your process to me. The goal here is to understand their entire process so you can find places your company can be of service, even if it's outside your normal offerings.

  Bob offers a great example. Their customer needed a rush job with next-day delivery. Bob checked in with their team and got agreement for a rare overnight assembly. The team worked double time and had everything ready at 11 a.m. the next day. The customer called them because their delivery service couldn't secure a truck. Because they were local—within two hours of the plant—Bob offered to deliver the product using their team and trucks.

  Bob made a client for life that day by solving the customer's immediate problem. They went a step further and offered to deliver all the customer's orders at an extra 12 percent markup on the order price. The customer immediately said yes. The third party was unreliable and later proved more expensive than Bob's upcharge.

- Were there times when we didn't meet your expectations? This one will be tough to hear. How have you let your customers down? Be open. Do not get stuck in your ego. Listen and take notes for valuable improvement ideas.

Another example is of a solo business owner who had a habit of missing deadlines. When she asked her customers for feedback, many pointed out this flaw. Accepting this, she not only acknowledged her mistake but also offered discounts if she was late again. This honesty and corrective measure rekindled trust with many of her clients.

- Can we reconnect again in a few months?

Remember, the goal during these conversations is to listen. The feedback might be hard to hear, but it's gold. Think like an investor in their business. How can your business elevate your customers to inevitable success?

Lastly, take the example of Bob. He divided his clients into four groups.

- ➤ Current
- ➤ New this year
- ➤ Past / Lost
- ➤ Prospects (not yet customers)

He saw more past clients than current ones, signaling a need for change. But there's also good news: Many current clients and new ones are coming in, indicating strengths in his approach.

By combining his new knowledge with his marketing analysis and brand ideals, Bob is developing a focused marketing strategy based on his newly acquired market intelligence.

* * *

Understanding and defining a company's brand, along with a strategic and data-driven marketing approach, are essential for achieving long-term business growth and profitability. By leveraging insights from CRM data and prioritizing customer needs over competition, businesses can develop effective marketing strategies that strengthen customer relationships and drive higher EBITDA. Use a hands-on approach with customers to stay in touch. Work to develop lifelong relationships by adding real value to your customers.

What market share do you have in the industries you serve, and specifically, what are the psychographics of the key decision-makers in each?

CHAPTER 12

Lever 7: Operations

Strategy without tactics is the slowest route to victory.
Tactics without strategy is the noise before defeat.

—Sun Tzu

So far, we've discussed the human factor, finances, and marketing, the three most crucial levers for increasing your EBITDA. Now, let's turn our attention to your company's **operations**: converting materials into finished goods, the products you sell. Service businesses convert processes and specialized labor into value-added services for clients. While each company is unique, manufacturing businesses add additional layers of complexity yet share many common processes.

Bob heads over to Millie's office, where orders are received. "Hi, Millie. How many orders have come in today?" he asks.

"I'm on the fifth now. Darryl just emailed three more," Millie said.

"What would you say is the easiest part of your job?"

"I suppose that's working with Darryl. He's a great salesperson. And he's also a great co-worker. He lets me know how many projects he's working on each day and the estimated quantities of the products. It makes it easier for me to look ahead at inventory so I can update Mary on the quantity and kinds of raw materials we need to purchase, so we're meeting our delivery timelines." Millie said.

"And your most difficult?" Bob asked.

"Finding clients in our system, updating their records, and putting the actual order into the system is the hardest. It takes roughly twenty minutes. Bob, the system's old, real old. I don't think we've updated it for five, maybe six years."

"What would you like to see?" Bob asks.

"Darryl enters his sales information into the CRM, but then he has to send it to me in an email. I'd love his CRM entry to automatically update my order system. It would free up so much time for me. Time I could use to analyze our orders in real-time for the latest trends." Millie said. "This would free Darryl up to focus more on sales calls and less on administrative tasks."

"Thanks, Millie. You've given me a lot to think about. Do you have a recent order that you sent down to the production floor?"

Bob steps onto the production floor, greeted warmly by everyone as he heads to the order tickets. He prints out the order sheet that Millie gave him. For this exercise, Bob decides to "staple" himself to the order, following it through each step of the conversion process. This is the source detail for the order fulfillment portion of the Profit Process Formula. When the order moves, he moves; when it stops, he stops. First, he confirms that Millie's order entry matches the quantities and inventory on the production request. Then, armed with a clipboard and pen, he applies the effective Management By Walking Around (MBWA) strategy.

For a moment, he pauses to admire the wood and questions why he would consider selling the business. Sawdust glitters in the sunlight as his hands shape the wood to artistic perfection. "Maybe," Bob thinks to himself, "I could just grow it to prime, have it self-managed and run, and let it live on to perpetuity, generating passive income for personal wealth. What a great legacy that would be … "

Cheryll approaches, "Hi, Boss. Excuse me, I need to get this maple lumber." She loads a 6-foot piece onto a dolly and heads back to the production line.

Bob follows her. "What are you doing there?" he asks, though he knows well, having built the company and "coincidentally" the lumber is for the order he is "stapled" to.

"We're planing the wood, cutting away imperfections and smoothing it to match the piece we're making, while leaving the edges of the wood natural, so the tree's shape comes through," Cheryll explains.

"Where does it go from here?" Bob inquires.

Bob takes notes and tracks the piece of wood through the entire process. Although he's done this countless times, this time he's focused on recording the specific distance between steps and the duration of each, paying attention to all the nuanced details of the order conversion process.

It takes Bob's order just over nine hours to move from order entry to inventory to a saleable table. He notes areas where inventory backs up, slows down for safety and quality, and machines that sit idle. More importantly, he creates a flowchart detailing the time required for each step.

By standardizing his products, Bob streamlined his production process, combining orders and boosting efficiency as his business grew. He hired Ralph as VP of operations to continue improving the already successful project. Ralph recommended implementing lean manufacturing. The lean manufacturing initiative aimed to remove waste, optimize operations, and integrate quality control directly into production.

Separating operations from inventory led to lower inventory costs and the procurement of more efficient machines, following a make-versus-buy analysis that showed a positive return on investment. Lean implementation significantly enhanced his efficiency, resulting in increased production, faster turnaround times, and reduced costs.

Bob had always supported batch processing, but now he's reconsidering. Is it the best method for moving inventory through the production floor?

Manufacturing operations can be managed in various ways. Businesses must schedule people, equipment, and inventory efficiently to move materials through various stages until they are packaged and ready for shipping. Batch processing, for example, involves producing 100 pieces per hour, then transitioning to a phase that can handle only 50 pieces per hour, resulting in inventory buildup, potential safety and quality issues, or minimal delays. The goal is to create an optimal inventory management system.

The goal, instead, is to line-balance your operation, ensuring items move through the process with minimal delays. To achieve this, create a flow chart for each stage of the material conversion process. Then use this to analyze what it would take to design a process for a one-piece flow, thus eliminating batch processing. Bob came up with the following example:

Basic Batch Process Flow

```
[Supplier]
  ↓ (3 weeks lead time)
[Receiving & Quality Check] — 1 hr 35 min
[Inventory: assign SKUs & shelve] — 45 min
[Order Entry (phone/email/online)] — 60 min
[Order Download to Factory] — 4 hr
[Material Retrieval - SKU 1] — 35 min
[Process Step 1] — 13 min
[Create SKU 1A] — 10 min 25 sec
[Combine SKU 2 + SKU 1A → Machine 2] — 25 min
[Subsequent steps → Final product]
```

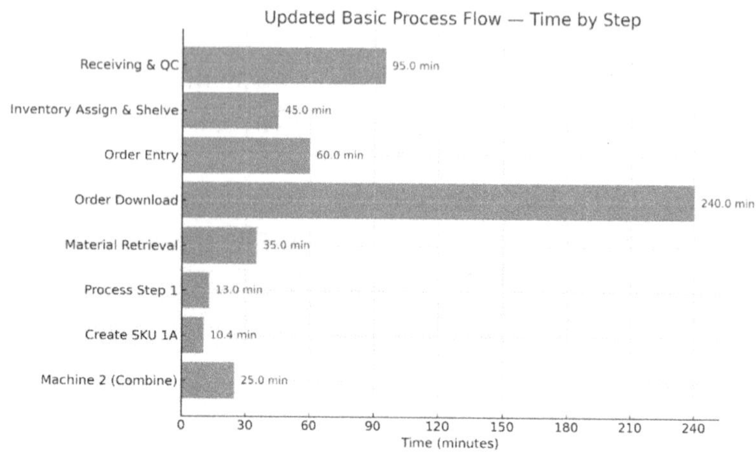

Batch-Oriented Flow

- Receiving & Quality Check — 95 min
- Inventory Assign & Shelve — 45 min
- Order Entry — 60 min
- Order Download — 240 min
- Material Retrieval — 35 min
- Process Step 1 — 13 min
- Create Stock Keeping Unit 1A — 10 min 25 sec
- Machine 2 (Combine) — 25 min

Total = 523 min 25 sec ≈ 8 hours 43 minutes

The process continues with each step creating a new product and Stock Keeping Unit (SKU) until the final saleable product is complete.

To maximize your EBITDA, revisit and reevaluate your process and production rates at each step. Understand the complete cycle and production rates at each stage.

- What's working?
- What's not?
- Where are the hold-ups?
- Are there steps that can be expedited?
- Are there processes that can be combined?

Examine the flow of employees across the production floor. Determine the optimal production size and layout to complete more orders and leave less unfinished product at the end of a shift. To optimize facility output, focus on the slowest part of the process and find ways to increase its throughput, a process known as line balancing.

Think of it as making one piece at a time: grab the raw material, process it, and hand it to the next stage, like a production bucket brigade. The slowest step determines the pace. Create a flowchart of the movement of people and materials, and make each step in the process as efficient as possible. Avoid unnecessary material handling. Think of Henry Ford's production assembly line for the entire process. Henry Ford's introduction of the moving assembly line in 1913 stands as one of the most transformative innovations in industrial history—and a perfect illustration of how process design can multiply performance. By breaking complex tasks into simple, repeatable steps and standardizing parts for interchangeability, Ford created a continuous-flow system that dramatically increased efficiency, reduced waste, and slashed the Model T's production time from twelve hours to just ninety minutes.

The genius of the assembly line wasn't merely mechanical—it was organizational. Each worker became a specialist in a defined task, allowing the entire operation to function as a synchronized system rather than a series of disconnected efforts. This principle—**streamlining process flow to unlock**

exponential gains in productivity and profitability—is at the heart of operational excellence.

See Bob's process improvement example that follows:

One-Piece Flow: Material & Information Path

```
[Supplier Delivery — Staggered, Frequent]
        ↓
[Inline Receiving & Quality Check]
(Immediate or ≤10 min per SKU)
        ↓
[Pre-assigned SKU & Point-of-Use Delivery]
(≤5 min)
        ↓
[Real-Time Order Entry & Auto Release]
(Integrated — <15 min)
        ↓
[Immediate Digital Order Release to Floor]
(No 4-hr lag)
        ↓
[Material Retrieval - SKU 1 at Workstation]
(≤5 min standard)
        ↓
[Process Step 1]
(13 min)
        ↓
[Automatic SKU Update / Label]
(≤2 min)
        ↓
[Process Step 2 — Combine with SKU 2]
(25 min or split into parallel ops)
        ↓
[Subsequent Steps — Flowing Continuously]
        ↓
[Finished Product → Pack & Ship]
```

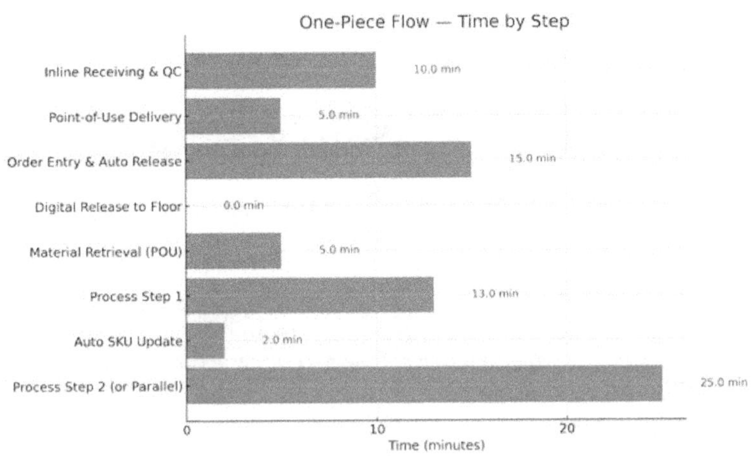

- One-Piece Flow
- Inline Receiving & Quality Check: 10 min
- Point-of-Use (POU) Delivery: 5 min
- Order Entry & Auto Release: 15 min
- Digital Release to Floor: 0 min
- Material Retrieval (POU): 5 min
- Process Step 1: 13 min
- Auto SKU Update: 2 min
- Process Step 2: 25 min

Total = 75 minutes

When comparing the before-and-after results of the operations analysis, the difference is striking: the **Batch Flow Total Time** is **523 minutes and 25 seconds**, while the **One-Piece Flow Total Time** is only **75 minutes**. This dramatic reduction highlights the significant efficiency gains achievable through one-piece flow. The key improvement opportunities between the one-piece flow and batch flow designs are illustrated in the graph below.

Key Design Shifts: From Batch to One-Piece Flow

Area	Batch-Oriented	One-Piece Flow
Material Arrival	Bulk deliveries every 3 weeks	Staggered, smaller, more frequent deliveries
Inspection	Entire shipment inspected before release	Inline sampling with immediate flow-through to operations
SKU Assignment	Centralized shelving and labeling	Pre-labeled materials delivered directly to point-of-use
Order Processing	Manual entry with delays	Real-time digital integration and auto-release
Information Flow	4-hour lag between order entry and release	Instant release to production floor
Retrieval	Pulled from central warehouse per batch	Point-of-use kitting, standard 5-minute retrieval
Processing	Queues form between steps	Immediate station-to-station transfer
SKU Updates	Manual creation and labeling	Barcode scan and auto-generation
WIP	Accumulates between steps	One-piece flow with minimal First In First Out buffers

* * *

Analyzing and optimizing your company's operations is essential for efficiently converting raw materials into finished goods, thereby maximizing EBITDA and long-term enterprise value. By systematically evaluating key processes—such as batch processing, one-piece flow, and line balancing—you can identify bottlenecks, eliminate waste, and improve synchronization between departments. Developing detailed process flowcharts not only helps visualize inefficiencies but also reveals opportunities to streamline production, minimize downtime, and elevate both productivity and product quality.

Furthermore, this analysis provides valuable insight into where new equipment, automation, or enhanced workflows can deliver the greatest return. It also supports better inventory management by optimizing turnover rates and reducing carrying costs. Beyond financial performance, operational improvements foster a safe, ergonomic environment that enhances employee morale, reduces injuries, and sustains long-term organizational health.

What equipment assets, technology, process layouts, and or suppliers can be added, deleted, or replaced with modern innovative work cells that can increase your quality, output, and reduce costs to increase your EBITDA?

CHAPTER 13

Lever 8: Asset Management

Do not save what is left after spending,
but spend what is left after saving.
—Warren Buffett

Assets are the equipment on the floor, software in the offices, and vehicles in the parking lot that keep your business running. Effective asset management is crucial for boosting your company's EBITDA.

"Hi Terry, how are things on the floor today?" Bob asked.

"That's not the question you want the answer to, Bob," Terry said.

"Now I definitely want the answer."

"The wood planer is down again. Production has stopped," Terry walked over to the wood planer. "It's the third time this week."

"Why am I just hearing about this now?"

"The wood planer is old. It's been giving us some trouble over the past year. We've managed to perform some in-house maintenance. We had a guy from Jim's Machine Repair work on it as well. He's retired and moved out of state," Terry said.

"Let me guess. We have no expert to maintain it?" Bob asked.

"Yes. That's where we're at."

"What do you need today to get back to work?" Bob asked.

"In the short term, someone will fix it," Terry said. "In the long term, a new machine."

Asset management includes identifying, documenting, and evaluating a company's assets and their returns on investment, and ranking them based on revenue generation, investment expenses, and maintenance requirements. Equipment needs preventative maintenance schedules to avoid urgent repairs.

Conduct a make-or-buy analysis before acquiring any asset. What's the price difference between making the parts and buying the parts? Producing parts is cost-effective if production costs are less than the price of buying them. Make sure to account for all costs, including freight, inventory carrying costs, extra stock to meet minimum order requirements, etc.

A make-buy analysis weighs multiple factors before any financial investment. First are repairs. To ensure swift, efficient repairs, plan by identifying skilled personnel or outside maintenance services. Second, a return-on-investment analysis should determine potential cost savings by considering all current and future process costs, as well as the asset's cost.

Boost efficiency by integrating new assets with your existing ones. Relevant assets encompass information systems, product manufacturing equipment, copiers, computers, and other process-oriented equipment. Consider building value and deterring competitors by investing in intangible assets (such as copyrights, patents, and trademarks) and leveraging legal protections for your intellectual property.

Your assets generate your revenue. Implement a system to routinely monitor the performance of every asset (both physical and intangible) to ensure optimal operation. Don't keep assets past their prime; upgrade when something better is available. Remember the sunk cost fallacy. Past investments shouldn't stop you from buying what you need now.

The sunk cost fallacy is the tendency to continue an endeavor or course of action based on poor investments (time, money, resources) rather than on current and future benefits. This fallacy can lead to irrational decision-making, as individuals may feel compelled to stick with a decision simply because they have already invested in it, even when it would be more beneficial to abandon it. Do not be a victim of this. If you can buy parts at a lower cost with equivalent or better quality than making them, conduct a review of why and how, and decide on the best, most profitable choice going forward.

When faced with several equipment options to invest in, manufacturers should apply a structured decision-making approach that goes beyond pure financial return. Each option should be evaluated against both quantitative and qualitative criteria: financial performance, strategic alignment, risk, and intangible benefits.

Financial metrics such as expected ROI, payback period, and total cost of ownership reveal economic efficiency, while strategic alignment measures how well the equipment supports the company's core objectives, such as expanding capacity, improving quality, or enhancing innovation. Risk and reliability factors assess uptime, vendor support, and technology obsolescence, ensuring that investments remain dependable over time. Intangible elements, including employee safety, ergonomics, and environmental impact, also influence long-term value.

By weighting and scoring each category—using a matrix or comparable framework—leaders can objectively compare options and identify which investment delivers the strongest overall contribution to EBITDA, operational performance, and sustainable growth.

CHAPTER 14

Lever 9: Cost of Sales

Revenue is vanity, profit is sanity, and cash is king.
—Alan Miltz

The ninth lever in our journey to boosting your EBITDA is optimizing your company's Cost of Sales (COS). Many business owners mistakenly believe that COS is the only route to a higher EBITDA. As we've seen, several levers ahead of this in the performance enhancement can have a broader impact on the business.

Bob printed out last month's expenses and the pipeline reports covering the next three to six months. He was particularly interested in the materials used to make their tables and furniture, such as wood, screws, and nails. Bob takes a red pen to his list, highlighting the expensive materials, then he stops.

He pushes back from his desk. There's more to making the product than just raw materials. COS is not a static number. Over the course of a month, inventory is used, new materials are purchased, and labor completes work in process and converts it to finished goods.

When calculating COS, you need to consider each of those, along with the inventory remaining at the end of the month. The formula is:

> Cost of Sales = Beginning Inventory Value (raw materials + finished goods) + Materials Purchased + Direct Labor Expense − Ending Inventory Value

This dollar figure represents the cost of creating products in the last month. We subtract the ending inventory because that becomes the beginning inventory for the next month.

Let's get a bit more granular.

Inventory encompasses raw materials, work-in-process, and finished goods. It refers to everything kept in the warehouse, including screws and the 6-foot table, which are in line to ship. Inventory is a fluid number. Parts will be used, new stock-keeping units will be built, and finished goods will be sold.

Direct labor is any human activity that directly contributes to the creation of the product. This covers the hours men and women spend working on the production floor. It excludes the time team members spend on website work, purchasing, marketing, bookkeeping, and other activities, as these are considered overhead.

Bob went to the production floor. Armed with the latest inventory list from Stan, he headed into the stacks to verify the numbers. He quickly discovered a discrepancy.

"Hey there, Stan. Can you come back here for a minute?" Bob stared at a pallet three shelves above him. "What's on that pallet? I can't read the stock keeping units on the label."

Stan climbed the ladder. "Bob, my reader isn't picking it up either. As you said, the label has been rubbed away."

"Come on down. Get a couple of the younger folks to pull it down from the shelf. We need to know what's in it."

Thirty minutes later, Bob's team unpacked the pallet, revealing three boxes each containing 10,000 1-¼" screws, seven boxes of sanding belts and discs, and twenty small custom side tables. The recovered items amounted to more than $5,000 in raw materials and finished goods that were missing from the inventory report.

"Stan, can you give Mary in Purchasing a quick call? How often do we buy 1-¼" screws?"

There is a science behind inventory management, and it turns materials into margin through control, flow, and precision. It is critical to know your beginning inventory, the right items in the correct quantities, to establish and follow procurement procedures. Mismanaged inventories result in lost money. Keep inventory separate from the work cell areas. Make sure to organize inventory extremely well in the warehouse by usage rate. Most frequently used inventory is stored up front to minimize inventory handling time. Store only the daily inventory levels required near the work cell site to produce the product for that day.

Inventory management is one of the most powerful levers for improving operational performance and profitability in any manufacturing environment. Inventory represents stored cash—cash that only becomes valuable when it is converted into finished goods and delivered to customers. When managed well, inventory supports smooth production flow, minimizes downtime, shortens lead times, and strengthens EBITDA. When mismanaged, it creates excess cost, disrupts schedules, and hides deeper operational issues.

Effective inventory management begins with visibility. A company must know what it has, where it is stored, and how fast it is moving. High system accuracy, disciplined cycle counting, and clearly defined material locations are essential. Organized warehouses, standardized storage, and clean material flow—from receiving to production to shipping—reduce wasted motion and ensure materials are always accessible when needed. Demand-driven replenishment ensures the right materials arrive at the right time without overstocking or shortages.

Optimizing inventory levels is a constant balance between service, cost, and cash. Too much inventory ties up working capital, hides inefficiencies, and increases the risk of scrap or obsolescence. Too little inventory causes line stoppages, expedited shipping, and missed customer commitments. Reliable forecasting, accurate Bill of Materials, and strong coordination between purchasing, engineering, and production planning are critical for maintaining this balance. Work-in-process inventory must also be tightly controlled; excessive WIP increases lead times, masks quality issues, and slows throughput, while well-managed WIP improves responsiveness and clarity.

Supplier alignment plays a major role in inventory performance. Consistent lead times, quality standards, and communication practices prevent disruptions and allow the manufacturer to plan with confidence. Scrap reduction, obsolescence control, and disciplined change management ensure that inventory remains current, useful, and financially healthy.

Ultimately, inventory management requires strong leadership oversight. Key performance indicators—such as inventory turns, days of inventory on hand, WIP days, accuracy percentage, service level, and supplier on-time delivery—must be reviewed regularly and acted upon with discipline. Companies that excel in inventory management create predictable operations, convert cash faster, and maintain a competitive advantage. In a world where speed, accuracy, and cost control define success, inventory is not just a support function—it is a strategic asset, essential to building a high-performing manufacturing enterprise.

Let's go back to our formula.

Cost of Sales = Beginning Inventory Value + Material Purchases + Direct Labor Expense – Ending Inventory

Example:

$10,000 Beginning Inventory + $3,000 Material Purchases + $7000 Direct Labor Expense – $7500 Ending Inventory = $12,500 Cost of Sales

This is the cost of sales for the past month.

You'll find this number on the income statement. Compare the cost of sales margin (Cost of Sales / Sales) across several months and quarters to uncover any trends.

Separate operations activity from inventory storage. Do not clutter the precious workspace with inventory storage. Organize work cells by the flow of product. Inventory accuracy is critical and requires diligent processes to maintain. Design processes to minimize and aim to eliminate material handling. In purchasing, consider using vendor-managed inventory to control procurement costs and outsourcing inventory management, as addressed in more detail in the next chapter.

What are your cost-of-sales margin per month trends, and what is the logic behind how your optimal inventory warehouse is laid out?

CHAPTER 15

Lever 10: Supplier Relations and Procurement

Coming together is a beginning, staying together is progress, and working together is success.

—Henry Ford

Your business's success hinges on selecting the right suppliers. These are the companies that provide your inventory, machinery, delivery drivers, internet systems, and anything that you rely on to produce and sell your product or service. Although price is a concern, other factors must be considered, including proximity, capacity, quality, and the quantity of supply.

"Jamie, can you come in here for a minute?" asked Bob.

"Of course. How can I help?" asked Jamie.

Bob points out, "Terry is using tape and rubber bands to hold the label printer together. We're way overdue for a new one. I just wish they'd told me sooner. Now we're rushing a supplier analysis, budget, and machine specifications to bid on a new one before downtime kills this quarter's profits. It is just a label printer; however, all our barcode readers need that printer for everything we produce!"

Jamie sighed. "I understand, Bob. Terry thinks he is doing you a favor by trying to fix it himself. The team doesn't see what it takes to get a new one. It's not like we can stop by Target and pick one up." Jamie smiled.

"I know. You're right. They do their best and more. It's just frustrating being under this kind of time constraint."

"So, how can I help?" asked Jamie.

"I'm analyzing the budget. Can you look at our supplier list for a few top choices? Speed and quality are our top requirements," Bob said.

Before you select a supplier, review your company's spending by commodity category. Classify all purchases and procurement funds by commodity, product, or service. Once your categories are identified, calculate the yearly and monthly spending totals. Knowing how much you can spend is essential to developing a process that's best for the company and the supplier. Remember to consider making versus buying analysis for critical purchases.

Procurement is more than selecting the latest model. It is a relationship, a two-way conversation that continues for the life of the contract and beyond. There are dozens of factors involved in purchasing a new product or service. Planning delivery frequency, quality, specifications, package quantity, packaging, and labeling are but a few of the critical factors for successful service. Supplier selection is serious business.

Whenever feasible, categorize and specify procurement items within current preexisting industry categories. For instance, to meet industry standards, manufacturers use American Society for Testing and Materials (ASTM) specifications to determine acceptable tolerances, weight characteristics, and chemical compositions of products. It is detrimental to develop your own standard specifications when the industry already defines them. To illustrate, the specifics of materials like steel (hot-rolled, pickled, and oiled), aluminum (killed, drawing quality, and commercial quality), and plastics (nylon content and regrind percentage) are precisely defined. The same applies to purchased services, including accounting, legal, and various IT services—defining your purchase specifications in alignment with the commodity or specific service commensurate with the industry is essential. You get what you order; therefore, know the proper specifications and align with existing industry standards when available.

Having defined categories and clarified specifications, we can now budget the annual spend for each. Now that you know your annual expenditure for each category, you can begin requesting bids. Selecting qualified suppliers sounds easier than it is. Consider the proximity to the location for efficient logistics, the manufacturer's capacity for efficient delivery, and the company's reputation in the marketplace. Note: continuity of supply is critical. Remember, supplier selection is serious business.

Many suppliers falsely claim to manufacture the products and services you buy when, in fact, they outsource. Although outsourcing isn't always bad, it can become problematic when your supplier passes your demands onto another vendor. A serious cost-time-distance analysis is required before deciding whether to go directly to the source or hire a middleman.

After identifying the top potential suppliers, send an official bid request to the decision-maker at each manufacturer. Often, a conversation is recommended to assess their knowledge and communication skills. Once we receive bids, we will evaluate them based on price, service levels, communication, response speed, and feedback quality. Plant tours and supplier visits are highly recommended after the top three are chosen, depending on the project price. Following that, a final agreement is drafted, detailing relationship terms, inventory specifics, delivery schedules, and quality standards. Managing and maintaining supplier relationships is critical. Regular communication, as in most other areas of life, is key.

Work with your supplier to proactively manage inventory by having them stock based on an accurate forecast for your items before actual demand, which offers security but also commits you to buying those pre-stocked items. Vendor Managed Inventory (VMI) is a supply chain management strategy in which the supplier takes responsibility for managing the inventory levels of their products at the customer's location. Instead of the customer placing purchase orders when stock runs low, the vendor monitors usage or sales data—often in real time—and replenishes inventory as needed to ensure optimal stock levels.

The goal of VMI is to improve efficiency, reduce stockouts, minimize excess inventory, and strengthen the relationship between supplier and customer. It shifts responsibility for inventory planning, ordering, and, in some cases, ownership of the stock until it is sold from the buyer to the supplier.

Key features of VMI include:

- **Data Sharing:** Customers provide vendors with sales, usage, or inventory data.

- **Vendor Responsibility:** The vendor decides when and how much to replenish.

- **Collaboration:** Both parties align on service levels, reorder points, and replenishment rules.

- **Benefits:** Lower carrying costs for customers, reduced administrative burden, improved product availability, and better forecasting for vendors.

In practice, VMI is common in industries where consistent supply and demand planning are critical.

Another useful procurement strategy is to leverage supplier contracts. Contracts can form the backbone of successful business relationships. These agreements are more than legal formalities; they are instruments of trust, accountability, and protection. A well-crafted contract defines the rules of engagement between a company and its providers, leaving little room for misinterpretation and minimizing the risk of conflict.

At the heart of these agreements is clarity. A contract should spell out exactly what goods or services will be provided, in what quantity, and at what quality standard. Delivery timelines, performance expectations, and pricing structures must be clearly documented. Payment terms—whether thirty days, sixty days, or milestone-based—should be explicit, and provisions for late payment or early settlement must be included.

Contracts also establish the boundaries of responsibility and risk. Warranties, guarantees, and indemnification clauses are used to protect both parties, while limitation-of-liability provisions ensure that no side bears undue exposure. In today's regulatory environment, contracts must also reflect compliance with industry standards, safety requirements, and environmental laws.

Another critical function of vendor contracts is safeguarding intellectual property and confidential information. Proprietary designs, processes, or data shared during the relationship should be protected through clear confidentiality clauses. When intellectual property is created during the engagement, the agreement must designate who retains ownership rights.

Equally important are the mechanisms for handling disputes and unforeseen events. Well-designed contracts specify whether conflicts will be resolved through mediation, arbitration, or litigation, and they identify which jurisdiction's laws will govern. Force majeure provisions account for events beyond the control of either party—such as natural disasters, political unrest, or global pandemics—that may temporarily excuse performance.

The best contracts balance structure with flexibility. While they establish firm expectations, they also allow room for adjustment as conditions change. Some agreements take the form of master service agreements or blanket purchase arrangements, designed to support long-term relationships with recurring projects or purchases. Others are short-term purchase orders, appropriate for one-time, low-value transactions.

Ultimately, vendor and supplier contracts are not just about protecting against risk—they are about creating a framework for enduring partnerships. When written with clarity, fairness, and foresight, they foster collaboration, build trust, and align the interests of both buyer and supplier toward mutual success.

Vendors are a critical element and the foundation for the products and services you provide to your valued customers. So select your vendor partners wisely.

What are the sourcing categories and dollars spent for the last three years of purchase history? How can a quality supplier selection process enhance your continuity of supply with a vendor-managed inventory contract?

CHAPTER 16

Lever 11: Products, Services, and Technology

Innovation distinguishes between a leader and a follower.
—Steve Jobs

Products: The goods or services a company offers to its customers. The quality, variety, and innovation of products directly impact customer satisfaction and market competitiveness.

Services: An action, process, or experience delivered to a customer that creates value without producing a physical product. It is the performance or expertise a company provides to meet a customer's need, solve a problem, or enhance an outcome. Services often involve human interaction, specialized knowledge, or technical skill, and their quality is measured by consistency, responsiveness, and customer satisfaction.

Technology: The tools, systems, and processes a company uses to produce and deliver its products or services. Implementing advanced technology can streamline operations, enhance productivity, and reduce costs.

> Implementing product and technology innovations can boost sales and improve operational efficiency, thereby enhancing EBITDA.

We're down to Lever 11. It might come as a surprise, but we're returning to the heart of your business: your offerings. The quality, variety, and innovation of these products directly impact customer satisfaction and market competitiveness.

Bob began his woodworking journey in the community college's woodshop, where he created custom pieces for his loved ones. To expand his business, he needed to move away from labor-intensive custom projects and create product lines for a broader market.

Product concepts are often the driving force behind new business ventures and expansions, but entrepreneurs may not fully understand the marketability of their ideas.

Time to do some research.

- Get feedback from your current customers if you have products on the market.
- Delve deep into identifying the features and benefits you have vs. what the market wants.
- Identify your key competitors and review their offerings for "ideas".
- Analyze the marketplace to differentiate your company from competitors based on your offerings, quality, and pricing.
- Look to social media for trends, innovative ideas, and opportunities for product improvement.

You have a few product ideas that could be successful. The plan is to test the viability on paper, then release prototypes to the marketplace to see what happens. It is kind of like fishing, you need to cast a lot and try different "lures" to see what gets the bites.

In market testing, services tend to be easier and less expensive to analyze than actual physical products. It usually comes down to finding the time and expertise within your company. Testing is also simpler. Select one or two clients who are your most frequent, best clients, and one or two who are occasional clients. Offer three price points: a budget-friendly option, a standard price, and a premium price. How many customers decided to get the service? At what price? What did they think about your new service? Ask and incorporate the answers. This should be considered a regular process in your business. Always be fishing because you never know when the "big one" will bite.

Creating and testing both physical products and software will require more time and resources. Companies often test early versions called beta versions to gauge customer interest.

My friend, who used to work in the infomercial industry, told me that those companies take a different approach to product testing. They produce just enough to film their commercial. We're only talking about the commercial here, not the orders associated with it. To launch their product, they invest between $10,000 and $25,000 in creating the minimum product, producing the commercial (often internally to save money), and buying airtime on specific stations. This is a small price to pay in the scope of their business.

They study the number of calls and sales generated by the commercial's airing. They'll only produce the product in large quantities if they reach their target numbers. If they don't, they cancel the customers' orders. Not a recommended strategy; however, a creative perspective to incorporate into your new product strategy.

Product & Service Features and Benefits are a high-leverage driver of business performance. One of the most powerful yet underutilized levers of business performance is the disciplined design and selection of product and service features. Most companies add features reactively—based on customer requests, competitor activity, or internal preferences—without evaluating whether those features truly create value. High-performing organizations take a strategic approach: they treat features as intentional decisions that must directly support customer outcomes, operational capacity, and long-term profitability.

The foundation of this lever is clarity on the core jobs the customer is trying to accomplish. Customers don't buy features; they buy outcomes—comfort, speed, durability, safety, prestige, efficiency, certainty. By understanding these desired outcomes, a company can map every product and service feature to a specific, meaningful customer benefit. This practice eliminates feature clutter, simplifies development, lowers costs, and ensures every attribute serves a purpose.

Once potential features are identified, the next step is to conduct a feature-benefit analysis. The organization evaluates each feature through a structured lens: What tangible benefit does it create? Is it essential or optional? Does it meaningfully differentiate us? What is the cost-to-benefit ratio? Will it improve our strategic position? This analysis helps eliminate internal bias and reduces the temptation to build beyond what the customer values. It redirects resources toward the features that matter most.

With analysis complete, companies use prioritization frameworks to select the highest-leverage features. A simple weighted scoring model—evaluating criteria such as customer demand, strategic alignment, competitive advantage, manufacturability, supply chain impact, revenue lift, and speed-to-market—brings discipline to the decision-making process. This ensures the business focuses on the critical few features that maximize both customer value and profit potential.

The final step is to translate the chosen features into a compelling value proposition that connects features to benefits and benefits to outcomes. High-performance companies articulate benefits clearly and concretely: stronger, longer-lasting, more ergonomic, more efficient, more reliable, more profitable for the customer. When articulated correctly, these benefits differentiate the offering, strengthen the brand, and create a powerful narrative that drives sales, loyalty, and margin growth.

When this lever is fully activated, organizations stop building products and services based on assumptions. Instead, they deliver offerings that customers truly value, sales teams can easily position, and operations can consistently support. The result is a cleaner product line, stronger margins, higher customer satisfaction, and a scalable, repeatable process for continuous product and service innovation.

A company committed to modern systems and processes requires a technology foundation that is integrated, scalable, and tailored to its unique enterprise needs. This means selecting secure cloud platforms, automation tools, and software ecosystems that align directly with how the business operates—not forcing the business to adapt to the wrong tools. The right technology should enhance existing strengths, streamline workflows, and unify functions such as operations, finance, CRM, and analytics into a cohesive whole. When properly matched to the organization, technology provides real-time visibility, reduces manual work, strengthens communication, and drives consistent execution. Ultimately, success depends on choosing and leveraging technology that fits *your* enterprise and supports efficiency, adaptability, and long-term growth.

To wrap things up:

- Know the real features and benefits the customers and prospects are demanding.

- Design and package your products and services to minimally meet what the customer wants and to exceed expectations to build product loyalty.

- Researching new products and services is key when considering company growth.

- Find the most cost-effective way to test the new product, service, or software.

- Leverage the right technology.

Work diligently to continuously improve the products and services you offer the market to avoid stagnation. Stay innovatively connected to what the market needs so your company continues to provide attractive sourcing solutions for your lifeblood—your customers.

What are the core features and benefits your customers need? What extra features and benefits would "WOW" your customers? How can you leverage cost-effective technology to stay organized and ensure the right information is available for quality decisions?

CHAPTER 17

Lever 12:
Continuous Improvement

It is not necessary to change. Survival is not mandatory.
—W. Edwards Deming

We've reached Lever 12. Congratulations! You've covered a lot: vision, strategic planning, human factor, financials, profit process formula, sales and psychographics, operations, asset management, cost of sales, supplier relations and procurement, and products, services, and technology. And now you're at the end, which is just the final step before starting the 12 lever process again at the beginning.

You need continuous reassessment and continuous improvement to sustain a business at perpetual prime. The work we've done is not static. Your vision could change, as will the strategic planning. People can leave your company, resulting in the loss of expertise. The financials may change due to unexpected costs or revenue. Your profit process flow chart may change as new systems are created and others are closed. I think you understand. The very act of moving through the 12 levers means things have changed and will continue to change. Change is inevitable, and getting comfortable with change is the catalyst for continuously improving your organization.

With Lever 12, Continuous Improvement, you return to the beginning, better for having learned what you did the first time around. It's time to start over, wiser than you were. Sustained growth requires repeating this process over and over, day after day, month after month, quarter after quarter, year after year, to ensure ongoing growth and optimize your Earnings Before Interest, Taxes, Depreciation, and Amortization (EBITDA).

It's like playing golf or any sport for that matter, practice makes progress. Progress is the fuel for continuous improvement. The journey through this book has been one of deliberate practice, discipline, and discovery. We have walked through the 12 levers that directly influence EBITDA—from vision, mission, and values to strategic planning, human capital, sales and psychographics, supplier relations, and beyond. Each lever is a tool, but together they form an **integration strategy** that, when consistently applied, builds momentum and multiplies value.

Optimizing EBITDA is not an event. It is not a single cost-cutting initiative, a one-time sales boost, or a quarterly adjustment. It is a discipline — a mastery. Just as a musician spends years training scales before creating symphonies, and an athlete practices fundamentals before breaking records, business leaders must engage in the same long-game of refinement. Mastery in business means building habits of clarity, accountability, and execution that compound over time.

The **12-Lever Integration Strategy**, at its core, is a system of **continuous improvement**. Every lever you pull creates feedback that informs the next decision, ensuring no aspect of your business is neglected. This is not a linear path but a dynamic integration—where measurement drives learning, learning drives refinement, and refinement drives greater results. Continuous improvement ensures the strategy never stalls; it keeps your business evolving, resilient, and competitive.

Leaders who embrace this mindset—which I refer to as The Way—begin to see EBITDA not as a static metric but as the living pulse of an organization's health. EBITDA reflects the discipline of execution, the foresight of planning, the creativity of innovation, and the resilience of relationships. By mastering the twelve levers and embedding continuous improvement into your integration strategy, you are not simply increasing your EBITDA; you may be in a position to command a higher multiple—you are creating sustainable value and securing the future of your enterprise.

This is the essence of mastery: the patience to stay the course, the discipline to refine the details, and the vision to see the whole. When applied to your business, these qualities elevate EBITDA optimization from a financial exercise to a legacy-building endeavor.

Your task now is simple but not easy. Practice mastery. Commit to the process. Use the **12-Lever Integration Strategy** as your guide. Continually strengthen each lever through continuous improvement until execution becomes instinctive, excellence becomes the culture, and growth becomes inevitable.

When mastery becomes your operating system, EBITDA value follows. And with it comes the freedom, resilience, and legacy that every entrepreneur and business leader seeks to create.

How do you measure progress?

PART 3

Measure. Master. Multiply— The Power Behind the EBITDA Report Card

CHAPTER 18

EBITDA Report Card

In God we trust; all others must bring data.
—W. Edwards Deming

You've done the work. You've moved methodically through the 12 Levers of Business Performance—clarifying vision, optimizing operations, improving financial fluency, aligning teams, and driving results. Each lever has been pulled, refined, and integrated to strengthen your company's value creation engine.

Now comes the ultimate test: **How do you know when you've succeeded?**

Use a leadership mindset for confidence, clarity, and sustained performance. One of the most common traps high achievers fall into is evaluating themselves against an imagined future ideal that continually expands as they advance. This future vision is useful for direction, but it becomes emotionally damaging when used as a measuring stick. The closer you move toward your goals, the more your mind elevates them, creating the illusion that you are always behind—even when you are accomplishing meaningful results. Measured this way, progress never feels like progress. Wins feel incomplete. Momentum stalls. Leaders begin to overlook how much capability they have already developed.

Backward progress measurement offers a far more constructive and accurate approach. Instead of judging your current performance against an ever-moving horizon, you evaluate yourself against the point where you began. This backward comparison reveals tangible progress: skills strengthened, decisions made, systems improved, obstacles overcome, relationships enhanced, and insights gained. All of these represent real, measurable advancements that forward-focused evaluation tends to ignore. When you look backward, you reclaim a sense of accomplishment that fuels confidence and renews your capacity to take on the next challenge.

This mindset is especially powerful within the Twelve Levers framework because each lever generates incremental improvement that compounds over time. Leaders who regularly acknowledge their progress stay resilient, think more clearly, and remain emotionally grounded through periods of change or complexity. Backward Progress Measurement reinforces momentum by highlighting what is working rather than fixating on what is still missing. It turns the leadership journey from a relentless chase into a disciplined, confident climb—one where evidence of growth becomes the foundation for the next strategic move.

When used consistently, this principle becomes an internal stabilizer. It allows you to maintain ambition without sacrificing well-being, to pursue excellence without diminishing your achievements, and to build your business from a place of strength rather than pressure. In short, evaluating how far you've come—rather than how far you have left to go—is one of the most powerful mental habits a leader can develop.

The answer lies in measurement. Without it, effort is simply activity without accountability. The *EBITDA Report Card* is your organization's scoreboard—a concise, real-time instrument that connects the levers of your business and translates daily actions into measurable results.

This chapter will show you how to **quantify progress**, evaluate management effectiveness, and ensure your business continues to perform at peak performance.

Why Measurement Matters

Data-driven management transforms instinct into intelligence. It replaces subjective opinions with objective truth. The *EBITDA Report Card* distills complex business activity into key insights you can act upon, helping you see trends, diagnose issues early, and reinforce behaviors that sustain profitability.

Just as a pilot relies on instruments, every leader must rely on accurate, timely data to stay on course. Numbers don't lie. They tell the story of how well your strategy, people, and processes are actually performing.

A Weekly Flash Report for Every Lever

The *EBITDA Report Card* is a **weekly flash report** that ties together sales, operations, purchasing, finance, and culture into a unified performance view. It measures both **leading indicators** (which predict future performance) and lagging indicators (which report past performance), allowing you to make real-time decisions.

Every business is unique, but the principles remain universal: measure what matters, review consistently, and act decisively.

Key Performance Indicators and Benchmarks

Every lever of your business must be anchored in meaningful metrics—clear indicators that reveal direction, current performance, and trajectory. KPIs are not abstract measurements; they are strategic levers that directly influence EBITDA, cash flow, and enterprise value. The most essential domains of measurement are Sales, Operations, Supply Chain, Finance, and Human Capital—each representing a core lever in the overall performance system.

Sales & Marketing (Lever 6: Psychographics & Sales Conversion)

Sales metrics show how effectively your organization converts opportunity into revenue. Indicators include booked orders, quote-to-close ratio, average deal size, new accounts, and customer retention. Strong companies grow 10–15 percent annually, convert above 25 percent, and retain over 80 percent of customers.

Operations & Manufacturing (Lever 7: Operations & Process Excellence)

Operational KPIs measure how efficiently your business transforms inputs into high-quality outputs. Key indicators include OEE, throughput, yield, scrap/rework, and on-time delivery. Best-in-class operations achieve OEE above 85 percent, delivery reliability above 95 percent, and rework below 2 percent.

Purchasing & Supply Chain (Lever 9: Cost of Sales & Vendor Relations)

Supply chain performance determines cost stability and production reliability. Important metrics include supplier on-time delivery, purchase price variance, inventory turns, and days of supply on hand. Healthy companies turn inventory more than eight times per year and maintain supplier reliability above 98 percent.

Finance & Administration (Lever 4: Financial Statements)

Financial KPIs reflect the ultimate outcomes of business performance. Gross margin, EBITDA margin, AR and AP days, and cash conversion cycle reveal profitability and liquidity. Strong financial systems maintain EBITDA margins above 15 percent, AR under 45 days, and cash cycles under 60 days.

Human Capital & Culture (Lever 3: The Human Factor)

People-based KPIs measure the strength and health of your culture. Indicators include turnover, absenteeism, safety incidents, engagement scores, training hours, and productivity. High-performance cultures maintain turnover below 10 percent, operate with zero recordable safety issues, and consistently elevate engagement.

Turning Data into Direction

Collecting numbers isn't enough. What matters is the **conversation** around them. The leadership team should meet weekly to review the EBITDA Report Card, interpret trends, and identify actions required. Each metric becomes a management dialogue: What's happening? Why? What's next?

This creates a **Closed-Loop Performance System** where every action leads to feedback, every piece of feedback leads to adjustment, and every adjustment strengthens EBITDA.

Measurement without interpretation is noise. Interpretation without action is a waste. The goal is alignment: data that informs, leaders that act, and teams that improve.

The Power of Consistency

When your business reviews its Report Card weekly, you build rhythm and accountability. Over time, trends reveal your leadership effectiveness, your operational maturity, and your organizational resilience.

Every metric tells a story. Together, they write your company's narrative of growth, discipline, and excellence.

Your reward for this discipline?

Predictability. Profitability. Peace of Mind. EBITDA Growth.

Your report needs to be tailored to your unique business requirements. The report card below is a representative sample of weekly metrics that need to be reviewed, discussed, acted upon, and used to evaluate trends in the management's effectiveness.

The EBITDA Report Card

The Weekly Flash Report, along with a monthly summary and Profit and Loss (P&L) comparison, will help you analyze how your monthly EBITDA changes.

		Preferred Results	Results
SALES	Responsible Party		
	Orders Placed	Greater	
	Shipments	Greater	
	Gross Margin	Greater	
	GM %	Greater	
	Finished Goods Inventory	Lesser	
	Finished Goods Inventory Turns	Greater	
	Domestic F.G.		
	Imported F.G.	Lesser	
	Inventory In Transit F.G.		
	Past Due Orders		
MANUFACTURING	Responsible Party		
	Labor Variance F/(U)	Zero	
	Cost Remainning in WIP F/(U)		
	Manufacturing Variance F/(U)		
	Indirect Labor OT	Lesser	
PURCHASING	Responsible Party		
	Vendor Returns	Zero	
	Raw Materials	Lesser	
	Raw Materials Turns	Greater	
	Domestic Raw Materials		
	Imported Raw Materials	Lesser	
	Inventory In Transit R.M.		
	Stanard Cost Variance F/(U)	Zero	
OPERATIONS	Responsible Party		
	Work in Process	Lesser	
	Work in Process Turns	Greater	
	Cost of Quality	Lesser	
	Headcount FTEs	Lesser	
	Sales / Emp	Greater	
FINANCE	Responsible Party		
	Operating Profit	Greater	
	Operating Profit Margin		
	Operating Cash Flow	Greater	
	EBITDA	Greater	
	EBITDA Margin	Greater	
	Working Capital Turnover	Greater	
ECONOMY	Housing Starts	Monthly	
	Unemployment Claims	Weekly	
	ISM Purchasing Managers Index		
	Stategic Items		

GOP (ATL Fed)	By Quarter	Estimate
		Actual

For each division/department, identify the key metrics, the department leader, and the team members responsible for gathering the data. For example, the sales department manages order placement, shipment processing, and analyzes order-to-shipment activity. Ultimately, gross margin and net sales are the key performance indicators for the sales department, as fulfilled orders drive the business.

Simplify data by using ratios to make meaningful comparisons to targets. You may not realize that hiring decisions, such as for a Request for Proposal (RFP) analyst, impact weekly numbers. The key is to carefully monitor the numbers and develop a keen awareness of subtle changes, such as new client orders resulting from the new RFP analyst.

Improving your company's EBITDA hinges on using the weekly flash report as a tool for implementing change.

The Weekly EBITDA Report Card, along with a monthly summary of Profit and Loss (P&L) comparison, cash flow, and the Robert Morris ratios and benchmarks, will help you analyze how your monthly EBITDA changes and guide you on what to do to get it to regularly trend higher and higher, pinpointing areas for improvement.

The Business Evaluation Scoring Matrix

Along with the flash report and EBITDA focus, here are six additional guidelines to prioritize your business's overall health as seen through investors' eyes. We refer to this as the Business Evaluation Scoring Matrix & Checklist. This further pinpoints universal value-enhancing areas to focus on. To evaluate a business's strength, sustainability, and overall value, these key categories should be carefully examined. Each area contributes to an organization's ability to grow, sustain profitability, and attract buyers or investors.

1. Growth and Profitability

A strong business demonstrates both historical growth and a clear, well-defined plan for future expansion. This includes strategies for market penetration, new product development, and competitive positioning. Profit margins should reflect efficiency and pricing power, maintaining levels that meet or exceed industry benchmarks. Consistent profitability is a sign of disciplined management and a sound business model.

2. Customer Base

The quality and diversity of a company's customers are central to its long-term success. A well-balanced customer portfolio avoids overreliance on any single account or industry. Longevity and client loyalty indicate that the business delivers lasting value. Additionally, customers with strong credit profiles reduce financial risk and improve predictability of cash flow. A business with diversified, loyal, and creditworthy customers is inherently more resilient.

3. Leadership and Industry Position

The caliber of management defines the company's trajectory. A deep and experienced leadership team—with clear succession plans—ensures operational stability and strategic continuity. Equally important is the health of the industry itself. Companies operating in expanding or innovative sectors are more likely to achieve sustained growth. Those that serve multiple industries or market segments mitigate risk by not depending on a single economic driver.

4. Product and Market Position

Businesses that maintain proprietary products, intellectual property, or unique value propositions hold a defensible competitive advantage. The diversification of gross profit sources—across product lines, customer types, or geographies—enhances stability. Market niche, positioning, and brand awareness further elevate perceived value. A strong brand identity creates recognition, trust, and pricing leverage, all of which are powerful contributors to long-term profitability.

5. Financial Health

Sound financial management underpins every thriving organization. Low or no debt, transparent financial reporting, and the absence of contingent liabilities indicate fiscal strength. Predictable maintenance and capital expenditure requirements are also essential to sustained performance. High-quality financial information—accurate, timely, and GAAP-compliant—provides decision-makers and investors with confidence. Interim financial results should confirm that the company's growth and profitability are consistent with its long-term objectives.

6. Presentation and Perception

Finally, how a business presents itself—its facilities, materials, digital presence, and overall professionalism—reflects the standards and discipline of its leadership. A clean, organized, and well-maintained appearance builds confidence with customers, suppliers, and potential acquirers. Perception often becomes reality; the way a company looks and operates communicates its internal health, discipline, and pride.

Summary

Together, these six areas—Growth and Profitability, Customer Base, Leadership and Industry, Product and Market Position, Financial Health, and Presentation—form the foundation of a comprehensive business evaluation framework. Organizations that score highly across all categories demonstrate not only operational strength but also strategic readiness for growth, investment, or acquisition. See the checklist below for an annual assessment of your company's compliance metrics with these universal standards.

Business Evaluation Scoring Matrix & Checklist

Category	Criteria	Description	Score (1–5)	Comments / Action Plan
1. Growth & Profitability				
	Growth & Growth Plan	Historical growth trends and clear future expansion strategy		
	Profit & Profit Margins	Sustainable profitability compared to industry benchmarks		
2. Customer Base				
	Diversification	Mix of customers minimizes concentration risk		
	Tenure	Long-term relationships indicating stability		
	Loyalty	High retention, repeat business, referrals		
	Credit	Quality of customer credit, low bad debt		
3. Leadership & Industry				
	Management Quality & Depth	Experienced leadership, bench strength, succession plans		
	Industry Growth	Healthy, expanding industry with favorable trends		
	Multi-Industry Distribution	Serving multiple verticals to spread risk		
4. Product & Market Position				
	Proprietary Mix & GP Diversification	Unique offerings, defensible gross profit sources		
	Market Niche & Position	Clear value proposition and market leadership		
	Brand Awareness & Identity	Strong branding, reputation, and recognition		
5. Financial Health				
	Debt & Liabilities	Low/no debt, no off-balance-sheet risks		
	Maintenance & CapEx	Reasonable, predictable future capital needs		
	Quality of Financial Info	Accurate, timely, GAAP-compliant financials		
	Interim Results	Recent performance supports growth narrative		
6. Presentation & Perception				
	Appearance	Facilities, materials, and brand presentation are professional		

Building a Business to Perpetual Prime with the 12 Levers

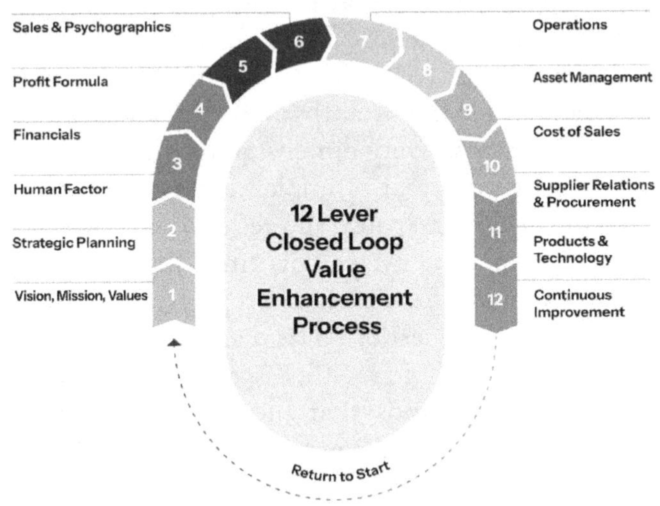

		2020	2021	2022	2023	2024	2025	2026	2027	2028	2029
EBITDA	Beginning Period	$	$	$	$	$	$	$	$	$	$
	Ending Period	$	$	$	$	$	$	$	$	$	$
EBITDA Margin	Beginning Period	%	%	%	%	%	%	%	%	%	%
	Ending Period	%	%	%	%	%	%	%	%	%	%
Notes											

As you reflect on the journey through the Twelve Levers of Business Performance, return to the Closed-Loop Diagram presented above. That visual is more than a model—it is your roadmap. It shows how each lever connects, reinforces, and amplifies the others in a perpetual cycle of improvement. By now, it should be unmistakably clear that this is a closed-loop, continuous-improvement system—one designed not just to organize your thinking, but to accelerate your results. When used consistently and intentionally, the Twelve Levers become the operating rhythm that guides every decision, aligns every team, and ultimately grows your EBITDA. This is your framework. This is your compass. And this is how you build a business that performs at its highest level, year after year. Boosting your EBITDA isn't something that happens overnight. It requires time, disciplined focus, sound judgment, and, most importantly, an integrated strategy that enhances value across every dimension of the organization.

After his first full year of implementing the Integration Strategy, Bob decided to pause and reflect before entering his next strategic planning cycle. This time, he came prepared with his workbook, which included reports, lessons learned, new ideas, and more questions. His plan wasn't perfect, but it was powerful: a record of growth, discovery, and momentum.

Bob now understands that increasing EBITDA isn't about chasing numbers—it's about building a business that operates at **perpetual prime**, guided by a three-to-five-year strategic vision and a deep understanding of how every part of the business connects. Each lever, when refined, reinforces the others. What follows are Bob's reflections on the twelve levers and how each one became part of his company's transformation.

The first lever—**Vision, Mission, and Values**—reminded Bob that clarity of purpose is the foundation of any thriving enterprise. Without a clearly defined vision of where the company is going, a mission that defines what it does, and values that guide its behavior, no organization can stay aligned for long. By revisiting and rearticulating these three pillars, Bob created a compass for decision-making. Every initiative—whether hiring, investment, or marketing—was now filtered through a simple question: *"Does this align with who we are and where we're going?"* When everyone could recite the mission and believe in it, performance followed.

Strategic Planning became a living discipline rather than a yearly event. Bob introduced quarterly review sessions to evaluate progress, identify gaps, and measure results. These sessions fostered collaboration, accountability, and agility. Strategy became a process, not a document—something measured, adjusted, and refined continually. Bob's mantra became: *"Plan, execute, measure, adjust."* Through this rhythm, strategic planning evolved from obligation into culture.

In the area of **The Human Factor**, Bob learned that human capital isn't just about staffing—it's about building the right team around shared purpose and trust. His VP, Harold, modified the Request for Proposal (RFP) process by creating an RFP analyst position, granting managers greater autonomy in selecting projects. Bob began evaluating team members not only for skills but also for attitude, accountability, and adaptability. Through cross-functional strategy meetings, he connected departments, sparked innovation, and strengthened culture. He also implemented succession planning for key roles, ensuring stability and long-term resilience.

With **Financial Statements**, Bob developed the financial fluency every leader must have. Understanding the balance sheet, income statement, and cash flow statement gave him a full picture of his company's health. He learned to read beyond the numbers—to connect cause and effect. Profits, cash flow, leverage, and liquidity were now viewed as interdependent signals of performance. By mastering financial ratios, Bob gained foresight. Financial reports became not static summaries, but strategic instruments guiding smarter decisions.

Through the **Profit Process Formula**, Bob realized that profitability is a continuous process, not a one-time achievement. He built a feedback system linking revenue, cost, and operations into a single performance loop. Each department tracked how its work influenced margins and customer outcomes. The loop—sales, production, fulfillment, feedback, and improvement—created accountability and clarity. Profit was now a shared responsibility, not just a financial target.

In **Sales and Psychographics**, Bob shifted focus from selling products to solving problems. He recognized that buying decisions are driven not only by logic, but by emotion and psychology. By understanding customer motivations, values, and lifestyles, his sales team became more empathetic and effective. He implemented CRM tools to analyze customer behavior through recency, frequency, and monetary value, identifying the best prospects for growth. Marketing became targeted and relational. The team no longer chased leads—they built partnerships.

Operations became another revelation. Bob "stapled himself to an order," tracing it from entry through shipment to see the full production flow. The exercise exposed inefficiencies and bottlenecks he couldn't have seen from behind a desk. He applied Management by Walking Around (MBWA) and transitioned from batch processing to one-piece flow, balancing workloads and reducing downtime. Operational excellence, he discovered, is the art of creating reliable, repeatable systems that continuously deliver value.

Through **Asset Management**, Bob evaluated every piece of equipment, every facility, and every investment. He began asking: *"Is this asset producing a return, or just occupying space?"* Idle machinery was sold, underused assets were repurposed, and key tools were upgraded for performance. Maintenance schedules and ROI analyses became standard practice. By proactively managing assets, Bob unlocked cash while increasing productivity.

Cost of Sales required a deeper understanding of where value was created and where it was lost. Bob traced expenses from raw materials through shipping, identifying unnecessary costs that didn't enhance customer experience. By renegotiating supplier terms, improving process flow, and adopting lean inventory methods, he reduced waste without compromising quality. His focus shifted from cost-cutting to **cost optimization**—ensuring every dollar spent generated value.

Supplier Relations and Procurement took on new meaning. Bob learned that vendors could be allies rather than adversaries. By fostering transparency, reliability, and shared innovation, he created partnerships built on mutual success. He invited suppliers into product development discussions, aligning incentives and streamlining delivery. The shift from transactional to strategic relationships turned procurement into a competitive advantage.

In **Products, Services, and Technology**, Bob embraced innovation as a continuous responsibility. He analyzed product lines for profitability and relevance, eliminating those that no longer served the mission. He invested in technology—from Enterprise Resource Planning systems to real-time analytics—that increased efficiency and accuracy. He began viewing technology as a force multiplier, enabling teams to achieve more with less effort. Innovation became a mindset, not a milestone.

Finally, through **Continuous Improvement**, Bob realized that excellence is not achieved—it is maintained. He introduced a culture of small, steady enhancements driven by his team's ideas. Daily huddles, improvement boards, and quarterly innovation challenges empowered employees to contribute to progress. Continuous improvement was no longer a department; it became the company's DNA. The business began to thrive not on perfection, but on momentum and progress.

As Bob prepared his workbook for the next year's planning session, he created a **Business Report Card** to track progress across all twelve levers. The framework enabled his team to establish SMART goals—Specific, Measurable, Achievable, Relevant, and Time-bound—that linked strategic intent with execution. His new paradigm became clear: *Work on the business, not in the business.*

After every initial investment of time and money, an owner must identify ways to create ongoing value. Bob's focus shifted from daily firefighting to long-term value creation—reducing inventory, improving factory efficiency, negotiating supplier terms, and elevating customer experience. These actions not only increased profitability but also inspired his human capital and increased the business's enterprise value. He began to view valuation as an ongoing management tool rather than a future event.

Many private company owners have most of their net worth tied up in their businesses, yet underestimate the importance of actively driving that value higher. Benchmarking a company's worth, understanding its value drivers, and reviewing them regularly should be part of every leader's operating rhythm. Valuation is not just about preparing to sell—it's about measuring growth, discipline, and stewardship.

In the end, after applying the principles of the Twelve Levers, Bob experienced a complete transformation—not only in his company's financial performance but in its culture and direction. He systematically strengthened every facet of his business: clarifying vision and values, tightening operations, optimizing costs, and building a leadership team capable of sustaining momentum without his constant involvement. With EBITDA substantially increased and the organization now running efficiently and autonomously,

Bob chose "Not to Sell" but to reinvest in his success. He decided to continue growing his business organically while also dabbling in growth through acquisitions. This dual strategy allowed him to expand intelligently, balancing stability with strategic opportunity. He focused on the parts of the business that truly inspired him while empowering others to lead and innovate from their core competency. By developing a solid succession plan and cultivating bench strength resilient to market shifts and workforce challenges, Bob positioned his company for long-term stability. Ultimately, he maximized his personal and enterprise wealth—and, with newfound clarity and confidence, began applying the same Twelve Levers framework to evaluate and integrate future business ventures.

Ultimately, Bob came to understand something profound: the real breakthrough wasn't just the growth of his business—it was the growth of *himself*. The 12 Levers had sharpened his thinking, expanded his awareness, and given him a new level of strategic clarity. He no longer saw businesses as isolated operations with scattered problems; he saw them as value-creation engines waiting to be tuned, aligned, and elevated.

Armed with this new intellectual capital—his earned wisdom—Bob felt a shift. Instead of simply managing his company, he began *mastering* the craft of business itself. And with that mastery came a bold new vision. He started looking outward, evaluating other companies through the lens of the 12 Levers, quickly identifying gaps, opportunities, and untapped potential beneath the surface.

What once felt complex now felt clear. What once seemed risky now felt achievable.

For the first time, Bob realized he possessed something rare—a complete, integrated framework that could transform any organization he touched. This gave him the confidence to explore new horizons: acquiring businesses, investing in undervalued operations, and applying his newfound understanding to create value far beyond the walls of his original company.

His journey had come full circle. By rebuilding his business, he had rebuilt himself. By mastering the 12 Levers, he had unlocked the next chapter of his life—stepping into a realm where he wasn't just growing companies, but shaping destinies. Bob wasn't merely creating value anymore. **He was creating futures. His own—and those of every business he chose to transform.**

Leadership Development as a Priority

Leadership Development is one of the most powerful levers for growing business value. When leaders expand their capacity, organizations expand their potential. Developing and leveraging your strengths is essential to optimizing EBITDA because your business will never outperform the capability, clarity, and courage of the people leading it.

Leadership development is the intentional, strategic process of cultivating the skills, abilities, and confidence of current and future leaders. It strengthens their ability to guide and inspire others, drive performance, navigate complexity, and adapt to constant change. This work happens through structured learning experiences, targeted coaching, mentorship, on-the-job practice, and consistent feedback loops that reinforce continuous growth.

The ultimate objective is simple and profound: **to become the best version of yourself**, personally and professionally.

What follows is an example of **Andreas Gfesser's "10 Best Leadership Development Journey Transformations"**—milestones, breakthroughs, and practices that shaped his evolution as a leader and can inspire your own path.

1. **Inspirational Future Clarifier.** To enhance my natural insight, I conduct best-practice research that aligns people with a meaningful purpose. Guided by a vision, fueled by virtues and values, leveraged by the wisdom of the past, and enhanced by the eradication of faults and weaknesses. The ultimate objective is to have limitless potential and abounding possibilities, co-creating a master plan aligned with our unique abilities.

2. **Compassionate Nuclear Bomb.** I have self-compassion. I contribute quality input to everyone I encounter. I compassionately comprehend what makes people tick. I learn how others want me to treat them. I understand the emotional atmosphere. I am a phenomenal pain detective. I deeply believe that every human experience contains a wealth of transferable wisdom; everyone has something to teach me. I increase the return on Human Capital. I transform others' failures into fuel for their success, and deliver positive autosuggestion to everyone.

3. **Goal Achievement Driver.** I optimize my finite time on earth by pursuing big, difficult, audacious goals. Goals provide attention, direction, and destination. I stay out of the gap and live in the gain by measuring my achievements backward. Pursuing SMART goals creates life and living.

4. **Results Maximizer.** I love leading by example. I illustrate the potential of results by highlighting the importance of one's life compass and the impact of flexible roadmaps on achieving goals. I encourage growth. I maximize results. I have been put on earth to empower others with deliberate action to make the world a better place. Radical focus and persistent effort are the transformational elixir of continuous improvement and sustainable progress. If at first I

don't succeed, I learn why, then simply try again a bit smarter!

5. **Optimal Solutions Creator**. Determining the best options to overcome obstacles is a natural talent. I pursue creativity, curiosity, and wonder to solve problems. I utilize a hyper-creative muse-inspired strategy for brainstorming. I prioritize *who* can implement solutions over *how* to solve them. I collaborate and never compete.

6. **Subject Matter Articulation Master**. I have a divine obligation to improve people's lives creatively with knowledge. I eloquently communicate the syntopical learning of complex concepts and ideas for simple comprehension. I deliver epiphanies to expand consciousness.

7. **Support System Game Changer**. I establish safe, constructive environments for conflict resolution. I equip people with empowering tools to resolve issues confidently and deliver negotiation power and prowess. I love creating game-changing support systems. I build trust, rapport, and comfort.

8. **Enthusiastic Equanimity Contagion**. I am always a calm, cool, collected, optimistic ray of sunshine. I love being a positive role model and a beacon of hope for what is possible. I continuously deliver encouraging perspectives. Once someone meets me, their life trajectory will be forever improved.

9. **Seasoned Mentor of Mentors**. I love mentoring people to develop sustainable, scalable solution paradigms. My objective is to align intentions with consciously enlightening actions to make the world a better place. I synergize our unique ability to positively leverage the compounding impact on resources. I develop one antifragile leader at a time with exceptional skill.

10. **Tactical Empathy Ace**. I love connecting, engaging, understanding, and guiding individuals to achieve win-win solutions. I naturally leverage this insight to fuel emotional intelligence. This inspires everyone to collaborate, be aware of, strive for, and cultivate habits that help people become the best version of themselves.

Andreas' leadership development habits culminated in a distinct and repeatable **Leadership Skill Implementation Process**—a sequence of strengths that, when activated in order, create profound clarity, momentum, and results.

He begins by stepping into the role of the **Inspirational Future Clarifier**, looking into the "crystal ball" of possibility and articulating a vivid, compelling picture of the future. With clarity established, he shifts into the **Subject Matter Articulation Master**, translating vision into confident, knowledgeable insights that others can easily understand and rally behind.

From there, he becomes the **Goal Achievement Driver**, channeling energy and focus toward the milestones that matter most. He complements this with his role as an **Optimal Solutions Creator**, generating relevant, practical, high-value ideas that move people forward. His ability to deploy **Tactical Empathy** gives him the precision of an **Ace**, enabling him to understand others' struggles and motivations at a deep emotional and intellectual level.

At key moments, he unleashes a **Compassionate Nuclear Bomb**—a powerful infusion of kindness, intensity, and belief that catalyzes action and inspires courage. As a **Support System Game Changer**, he stands shoulder-to-shoulder with those he leads, offering stability, insight, and unwavering presence.

His experience makes him a **Seasoned Mentor of Mentors**, guiding not only individual leaders but also those who influence entire teams and organizations. His presence generates an **Enthusiastic Equanimity Contagion,** bringing a blend of calmness, optimism, and grounded enthusiasm that elevates everyone around him. Finally, he channels his strengths as the **Results Maximizer,** consistently uncovering aligned actions that drive the best possible outcomes.

In the end, knowing your strengths as a leader—and intentionally cultivating them—is a defining virtue. Equally important is the wisdom to delegate tasks that leverage your weaknesses to team members whose strengths complement your own. This is emotional intelligence in action. And it is foundational to building a world-class team of value-creation professionals capable of driving continuous improvement and expanding enterprise performance. Never stop evolving to become the best version of yourself!

APPENDIX A

Definitions

Amortization: An accounting method used to systematically allocate the cost of an intangible asset over its useful life, such as a trademark or patent.

Balance Sheet: a financial statement that provides a snapshot of a company's financial position at a specific point in time, detailing its assets, liabilities, and shareholders' equity. It illustrates what the company owns and owes, as well as the invested capital, structured around the fundamental accounting equation:

Assets – Liabilities = Shareholders' Equity

Balance Sheet: The balance sheet helps stakeholders assess the company's liquidity, solvency, and overall financial stability.

Branding: The process of creating a unique image and identity for a product or company through the use of distinctive names, symbols, designs, and messaging. It involves developing a consistent image and reputation that sets the brand apart from competitors and resonates with the target audience. Effective branding helps build recognition, trust, and loyalty among consumers, ultimately enhancing the brand's perceived value and driving business growth. Key elements of branding include brand name, logo, tagline, visual design, brand voice, and overall customer experience. Branding targets customer emotions. Know your customer's lifetime value.

Cash Flow, Operating Cash Flow, and Free Cash Flow:

Cash Flow is the company's cash inflows and outflows. It provides an overall view of the company's liquidity and cash management.

Cash Flow = Revenue − Operating Costs +/− Investing Costs and Income − Financing Debt

Operating Cash Flow is the portion of cash flow derived specifically from the company's day-to-day operations, such as selling products or providing services. It does not include income generated through investments. Operating Cash Flow assesses the company's ability to generate sufficient cash to sustain operations and meet short-term obligations.

Operating Cash Flow = Revenue − Operating Costs − Investment (Interest) Income − Financing Debt

Free Cash Flow is a specific measure of cash flow that focuses on the cash left over after a business pays for its operating expenses and capital expenditures, such as machinery and vehicles. It focuses on discretionary cash remaining after necessary expenditures. Free cash flow represents the cash available to shareholders, investors, or for reinvestment in the business. It's a critical measure of a company's financial health and ability to generate value. To put it succinctly, free cash flow is the net amount of cash left over after a well-run organization's operations.

Free Cash Flow = Operating Cash Flow – Capital Expenditures (CapEx)

Cash Flow Statement: A financial statement that details a company's cash inflows and outflows over a specific period, categorized into operating, investing, and financing activities. It provides insight into the company's liquidity and cash management, helping stakeholders assess its financial flexibility and ability to generate cash. While this statement doesn't specifically note free cash flow, it can be calculated from it.

Competition: Other businesses offering similar products or services within the same market. Effective understanding and strategic management of competition can help a business maintain or increase its market share, enhance customer satisfaction, and ultimately positively impact EBITDA. Competition is a great tool for observing market trends.

Corporate Venture Capital: Corporate venture capital divisions of large corporations invest in smaller companies that align with their strategic goals. These buyers might look for businesses that complement their core operations and offer opportunities for collaboration or innovation.

Cost of Sales: The direct costs attributable to the production of goods sold by a company, including purchased goods, materials, and labor. Lowering the cost of sales can directly increase EBITDA. This is a critical area for managing inventory turnover.

Customer Lifetime Value (CLV): A metric that estimates the total revenue or profit a business can expect from a single customer over the course of their relationship. CLV is critical for making informed decisions about customer acquisition, retention strategies, and overall resource allocation.

Depreciation: An accounting method used to allocate the cost of a tangible asset, such as a truck or building, over its useful life. This systematic allocation reflects the asset's consumption, wear and tear, or obsolescence.

Earnings: The net income or profit of a company after all expenses have been deducted from total revenue. It is calculated as Total Revenue minus Total Expenses, which include the cost of goods (COGS), operating expenses, interest, taxes, and other expenses.

EBITDA: Earnings Before Interest, Taxes, Depreciation, and Amortization. This metric represents the company's earnings before interest, taxes, depreciation, and amortization. It offers insight into a company's overall financial performance and is commonly used as a standardizing metric to compare businesses apples-to-apples within the same industry, providing a clearer view of operational profitability than net income. EBITDA measures a company's operational profitability, while free cash flow represents the actual cash generated after accounting for capital expenditures and changes in working capital. While EBITDA provides insight into core business performance, free cash flow offers a clearer picture of the cash available for growth, debt repayment, or shareholder distributions. Cash is King.

EBITDA Margin: A financial metric that measures a company's operating profitability as a percentage of its total revenue. It is a key indicator of financial health and operational efficiency. The EBITDA Margin is calculated by dividing EBITDA by Total Revenue and then multiplying the result by 100 to express it as a percentage. EBITDA and EBITDA Margin are standardized financial metrics used to compare the operational profitability and efficiency of companies within the same industry by excluding the effects of financing, accounting, and tax differences.

Family Offices: Family offices manage the wealth of high-net-worth families and often invest in private companies. They look for stable, profitable businesses that provide steady returns and might be interested in companies with $5 million in EBITDA due to their lower risk and established performance.

Financials: The financial statements and records, including income statements, balance sheets, and cash flow statements, provide a comprehensive overview of a company's financial health. Accurate financials are crucial for calculating and improving EBITDA.

Human Capital: The skills, knowledge, and experience possessed by an organization's employees. Effective management of human capital can enhance productivity and profitability, positively impacting EBITDA. Always hire talent to grow the business.

Income Statement: Also known as a profit and loss statement (P&L), the Income Statement is a financial document that summarizes a company's revenues, expenses, and profits or losses over a specific period. It provides insight into a company's financial performance by showing how revenue is transformed into net income.

Individual Buyers: Private individuals who purchase businesses, typically small to medium-sized enterprises (SMEs), for personal investment purposes. These buyers may be entrepreneurs seeking to run their own businesses, experienced professionals looking to leverage their industry knowledge, or investors seeking to diversify their portfolios. Individual buyers often finance their purchases through a combination of personal savings, loans, and, in some cases, seller financing. They are usually involved in the business's day-to-day operations post-acquisition and aim to grow the company and enhance its profitability.

Interest: The cost incurred from borrowing funds (loans and liens) and the income earned from invested cash reserves held in the bank.

Investment Bankers: Professionals who work for investment banks, which are financial institutions specializing in large and complex financial transactions. Their roles include advising companies on mergers and acquisitions (M&A), underwriting new debt and equity securities for corporations, facilitating the sale of securities, and helping companies navigate the process of going public through initial public offerings (IPOs). Investment bankers provide expert financial analysis, valuation services, and strategic advice to help clients achieve their financial and business objectives.

Key Performance Indicators (KPIs): Measurable values that demonstrate how effectively an organization is achieving its key business objectives. KPIs are used at various levels of an organization to evaluate success in achieving targets. They are essential tools for monitoring and managing performance, guiding strategic and operational decisions, and driving continuous improvement.

Lifecycle of a Business: The stages a business goes through from inception to growth, maturity, and eventually, either renewal or decline. Understanding these stages helps plan and optimize EBITDA at each phase.

Marketing: The activities and strategies a company uses to identify and target specific markets and then promote and sell its products or services. Effective marketing can boost sales and revenue, positively affecting EBITDA.

Multiples: A financial ratio used by private equity firms and more sophisticated buyers in general to determine the valuation of a company. The multiple is applied to the company's EBITDA to estimate its purchase price. The multiple range varies by industry. In this book, we use multiples ranging from 4x to 8x. For example, a private equity firm might pay four times a business's EBITDA to determine its purchase price.

Operations: The day-to-day activities involved in running a business. Efficiently managing operations can reduce costs and increase earnings, thereby boosting EBITDA.

Private Equity Firms: Investment management companies that provide capital to private companies or execute buyouts of public companies, transforming them into privately held entities. These firms typically acquire a significant or controlling stake in companies to restructure, improve operations, and increase profitability, before exiting through a sale, IPO, or merger. Private equity firms often use a combination of debt and equity to finance their acquisitions and focus on mature companies with established business models and large growth potential.

Products: The goods or services that a company offers to its customers. The quality, variety, and innovation of products directly impact customer satisfaction and market competitiveness.

Standard Industrial Classification Code (SIC): A system for classifying industries by a four-digit code. The SIC system categorizes businesses by primary industry and the nature of their operations. Businesses use SIC codes to organize and analyze economic data across different sectors of the economy. Each SIC code corresponds to a specific industry, making it easier to compare companies within the same industry and gather statistical data on economic activities.

Stock Keeping Unit (SKU): A number or combination of numbers and letters that is unique to a specific inventory item. This encompasses all raw materials and items produced at the various steps in the production process. Companies must carefully manage the SKUs to ensure accurate inventory accounting. Inventory is money. Managing it effectively will grow EBITDA.

Taxes: Government-imposed charges on earnings, which vary by location. Adding taxes back into Earnings in the EBITDA calculation standardizes profitability comparisons across companies in different regions.

Technology: The tools, systems, and processes a company uses to produce and deliver its products or services. Implementing advanced technology can streamline operations, enhance productivity, and reduce costs. Implementing product and technology innovations can boost sales and improve operational efficiency, thereby enhancing EBITDA.

Venture Capital Firms: Specialized investment firms that provide funding to startups and early-stage companies with high growth potential. These firms pool capital from various investors to create venture capital funds, which they use to invest in promising startups in exchange for equity. Venture capital firms not only supply financial resources but also offer strategic guidance, networking opportunities, and operational support. They focus on sectors with high growth potential, such as technology, healthcare, and biotechnology, aiming to generate significant returns through successful exits, including IPOs and acquisitions.

APPENDIX B

References and Books

Stock and Business Valuation

The Intelligent Investor (Benjamin Graham)

Security Analysis (Benjamin Graham & David Dodd)

The Little Book of Valuation (Aswath Damodaran)

Business Analysis and Valuation (Krishna Palepu)

Modern Investment Theory (Robert Haugen)

Value Investing – From Graham To Buffett and Beyond (Bruce Greenwald)

Determining Value (Richard Barker)

The Theory of Investment Value (John Burr Williams)

Equity Asset Valuation (Jerald E. Pinto, Elaine Henry, Thomas R. Robinson, John D. Stowe)

Narrative and Numbers (Aswath Damodaran)

Valuation – Measuring and Managing The Value of Companies (McKinsey & Company)

Manufacturing

How To Implement Lean Manufacturing (Lonnie Wilson)

The Toyota Way: 14 Management Principles from the World's Greatest Manufacturer (Jeffrey Liker)

"Faster, Better, Cheaper" in the History of Manufacturing: From the Stone Age to Lean Manufacturing and Beyond (Christoph Roser)

The Innovator's Dilemma: When New Technologies Cause Great Firms to Fail (Clayton M. Christensen)

The Design of Everyday Things (Don Norman)

APPENDIX C

Digitize Due Diligence Files

Get a head start on value enhancement by staying organized and addressing key Considerations in Corporate Due Diligence for mergers and acquisitions. Seriously consider digitizing the following files for a centralized location for these key documents:

- **Intellectual Property.** Are there any IP issues that could block the company from practicing or fully utilizing the potential of any technological breakthrough? If so, are there any workaround options?

- **Human Resources.** Consideration should be given to all HR issues, including HR handbooks and guidelines.

- **Legal risks of commercialization.** This can range as broadly and as deeply as the ocean and is highly dependent on other issues uncovered during due diligence.

- **Long-term product integrity.** Is the business one that is sustainable? Is there a profit sanctuary, and is the product robust?

- **Development issues.** What types of code and/or development issues or hurdles remain? If some exist, is there a plan and timeline for their completion?

- **Integration of third-party IP.** If third-party IP is required for the business to be sustainable, what are the legal and financial liabilities of using external IP within the business?

- **In-person interviews with software developers.** This is always helpful and could lead to a separate list of resources to support internal operating systems.

- **Third-party patent clearance study.** In some cases, having a third-party patent attorney review potential IP issues will be absolutely necessary. Better to pay a little up front rather than getting slapped with a huge lawsuit down the road.

- **Inbound/outbound license agreements.** Depending on how services flow, there are often expenses with inbound and outbound software license agreements. Knowing the process can sometimes open up many other questions. Due diligence questions must be asked regarding both pricing and processes.

- **Source-code escrow release agreements.** What about the source code? How will it be transferred in the event of divestiture? How is it currently being transferred via employees and contractors?

- **Potential unwritten side deals.** Are there other deals, offers, freebies, giveaways, or agreements that are outside the scope of what the company initially represented? If so, what is outstanding?

- **Company articles of incorporation and corporate bylaws.** These are generally pretty boilerplate, but they will be helpful in determining the organization's official structure.

- **List of pending and/or threatened lawsuits against the company.** Get the dirty laundry out and shake it out.

Due Diligence on Company Employees

- Existing employment issues
- Golden parachute
- General current and potential retention and compensation issues
- Non-compete covenants
- Stay bonuses
- New employment recommendations

Financial Due Diligence

- Annual financial statements for five years (income statement, balance sheet, cash flow statements)
- Reconciliation of federal tax returns to annual income for the preceding five years
- List of annual sales by product category, including category, revenue, and gross margin
- List of annual revenue by marketing channel
- List of standard product lines, including regularly stocked items, along with the most recent cost per unit

The more the deal team knows about the target company's industry, the better positioned it is to demonstrate the company's true value.

ACKNOWLEDGMENTS

I wish to begin by acknowledging my father, **Anton**, whose remarkable entrepreneurial ability, natural leadership, and immense effectiveness in communicating and dealing with people have profoundly shaped my life. His rough but funny sense of humor brought warmth and levity to even the most challenging situations. His vision, courage, and ability to build and lead have been an enduring source of inspiration in my life and in the pages of this book.

To my mother, **Katherina**, thank you for your boundless love and support for as long as I can remember, and for the great friendship we have developed over the years. Your unwavering presence has been a constant source of strength and joy, and your influence has been deeply felt in every step of my journey.

I want to express my deepest gratitude to my wife and best friend, **Linda**, who has illustrated what true strength, support, and partnership look like. Your unwavering love and encouragement have been the foundation upon which this work was built. Your belief in me has fueled this journey, and your patience during countless late nights has been nothing short of extraordinary. You have stood by my side through every season, and for that, I am profoundly grateful.

To my son, **Ryan**, your natural creative ability and deep wisdom about how people interact in the world continually inspire me. Your insight and perspective are well beyond your years, and they remind me of the power of imagination and discernment working hand in hand.

To my daughter, **Justina**, your loving, organized ambition beautifully illustrates your focus on what a balanced and intentional life looks like. Your clarity of purpose and unwavering sense of direction are qualities I deeply admire and celebrate.

I also wish to acknowledge my brothers and partners, whose influence and collaboration have shaped both my personal and professional journey.

To **Anton**, thank you for your many years of leadership, guidance, and for being a great mentor throughout my career and life. Your wisdom and example have profoundly shaped my path. You have strengthened me in ways few ever could, cultivating in me more antifragility skills than anyone else. Your influence has been foundational, enduring, and deeply appreciated.

To **Stefan**, thank you for your continued encouragement and for challenging me to grow into a true leader. Your relentless drive and high standards have sharpened me in ways few others could. Over the years, our relationship has grown beyond professional collaboration into one of my deepest and most valued friendships, something I cherish greatly.

To **Martin**, your depth, breadth, and width in how you approach life are extraordinary. You possess a wonderful sense of humor and a light-hearted spirit that brings joy to those around you, yet beneath that lies a capacity and ability deeper than any ocean on earth. Your servant leadership and the unique way you bring people together with both warmth and wisdom are qualities I deeply admire and respect.

I would like to extend my sincere appreciation to **Stephanie** for her many hours of editing and for keeping me focused and organized. Without her steadfast support, this project could not have come to fruition.

To all of the **amazing manufacturers** I have the privilege of representing, thank you for illustrating the challenges and triumphs of manufacturing in extremely competitive environments. Your dedication and resilience are both humbling and inspiring.

To all the **service-sector businesses** I have had the honor of serving, helping you manifest into great organizations has been both a privilege and a learning journey. Your insight and unique perspectives on commerce have helped shape some of the greatest lessons that inform the ideas within these pages.

I also wish to thank all of my **amazing coaching clients** who have courageously expressed their vulnerability and their desire to become the best version of themselves through sacrifice, growth, and the willingness to dig deep to discover their true identities. Your commitment to leveraging your strengths to become extraordinary leaders has been both humbling and inspiring, and it has been an honor to walk alongside you on your journeys.

I wish to thank the **Executive Leadership Forum**, which has operated as my own personal board of advisors, guiding me through personal, business, and family matters with wisdom, honesty, and care. The collective life experience of these gentlemen has profoundly enriched my own journey. By openly sharing their stories, lessons, and perspectives, they have enabled me to extract timeless wisdom and apply it meaningfully to my life. It has truly been *steel sharpening steel* in the way we have interacted, and their insight and camaraderie have contributed immense value to the ideas and frameworks in this book.

I also wish to acknowledge all the **teachers and professors** who have helped shape the paradigm of my worldview. I am deeply grateful for the service they have provided and the knowledge, perspective, and discipline they instilled in me along the way.

Each of you has played a meaningful role in my life and in the principles expressed within these pages. For that, I am sincerely grateful.

PARTING WORDS
FROM THE AUTHOR

The Architecture of Purpose, Creativity, and Perpetual Prime

As you turn the final pages of this book, I want to share the deeper story behind its creation—because this work is more than a framework. It is the culmination of a lifetime of searching, learning, building, and evolving. It reflects not only what I know about business, but also what I've come to understand about life, purpose, and the pursuit of mastery.

The journey began not as a manuscript but as an intuition—a quiet idea living somewhere between experience and inspiration. It grew from notes taken on airplanes, ideas scribbled in margins, conversations in factories and boardrooms, and decades spent building and rebuilding organizations. What you've just read is the distilled essence of that journey: my attempt to articulate a clear, practical, universal philosophy for how leaders create value, unlock potential, and build businesses that endure.

And in writing it, something unexpected happened.

I discovered clarity—not just about business, but about myself.

Why I Am Here

I am the Founder of Crossroads Business Partners and the creator of *The Twelve Levers of Business Performance*. But titles alone do not define purpose. My deeper mission is simple yet profound: to serve God, live fully in the present, and grow continually through gratitude, serenity, exploration, and love.

I believe true nobility is not being superior to others, but becoming superior to my former self. Each day, I strive to evolve spiritually, mentally, and physically toward the highest version of who I am meant to be. This book is part of that evolution.

Over the course of my life and career, I've learned that mastery is never accidental. It emerges from clarity, alignment, and disciplined growth. My unique ability—my superpower—is expanding what is possible. I see inspirational futures with uncommon clarity, articulate them with precision, and help others align their natural talents with deeper purpose.

This is the same philosophy that shaped the Twelve Levers.

The Twelve Levers as a Universal Architecture of Growth

These levers—Vision, Leadership, Strategy, Financials, Sales, Operations, Human Capital, Cost of Sales, Asset Management, Supplier Relations, Customer Experience, and Continuous Improvement—are more than operational concepts. They reflect the universal laws that govern both business and life.

When they align, something extraordinary happens: a state I call Perpetual Prime—continuous progress, sustainable success, and the ability to evolve without losing momentum.

In creating this system, I discovered that I wasn't just documenting principles; I was giving form to a way of seeing the world. A way of integrating faith, discipline, leadership, and creativity into a coherent philosophy of growth.

The Leader Behind the Framework

My leadership philosophy is rooted in faith, responsibility, and balance.

> I build my body as a vessel.
> I train my mind to master emotion.
> I align my spirit with divine order.
> I lead with integrity and care deeply for the welfare of my family, my partners, and every person God places in my path.

I have learned that failure is not final; it is formative. I am either winning or learning. With fierce trust in God's purpose, I move forward with courage, calmness, and clarity.

Each evening, I reflect on three wins, plan three for tomorrow, and release all burdens to God—waking each morning renewed and unencumbered. I commit to making my future greater than my past, my purpose greater than my profit, and my contribution greater than my reward.

The Creative Journey That Built This Book

Bringing this book into the world required more than knowledge. It required creativity—true creativity, the kind that transforms intuition into structure, experience into principle, and insight into something others can use.

That process has been one of the most rewarding experiences of my life. It allowed me to see the architecture of my own thinking with clarity. It helped me understand not only what I know, but why I know it. It reinforced my conviction that business is not merely a mechanical system—it is a living organism shaped by vision, leadership, communication, accountability, and the discipline to grow.

This project affirmed something essential about creativity: that the act of creating is itself transformative.

A Final Word to You, the Reader

If you have reached this point, then you, too, are on a path of becoming—striving not only to build a better business but to become a better leader.

My hope is that these Twelve Levers give you more than strategy. I hope they give you a new way to see: your business, your team, your decisions, and your future.

But more importantly, I hope they help you see yourself more clearly—your strengths, your purpose, and your role as the architect of what comes next.

The real work begins now.

Your next chapter will be written not by reading these ideas but by *applying* them—by aligning your talents, elevating your thinking, and leading with faith, courage, and clarity.

Through my consulting, coaching, speaking, and writing, I will continue helping others unlock their own Twelve Levers—to expand what is possible in their businesses and in their lives.

My mission is to raise the quality of consciousness in every life I touch, extract meaning and order from chaos, and guide leaders toward the harmony of purpose, growth, and faith.

Thank you for allowing me to share this journey with you. May your path forward be bold, intentional, aligned—and filled with the quiet confidence that comes from knowing God is guiding your steps.

—Andreas Gfesser
Founder, Crossroads Business Partners
Creator, The Twelve Levers of Business Performance

Lead. Grow.
Maximize Value.

Leadership development isn't a program—it's a strategic investment in your future.

Through executive coaching, mentorship, and real-world leadership experiences, Andreas Gfesser empowers leaders to gain the clarity, confidence, and capability to inspire teams, drive performance, and lead with purpose.

Unlock Your Leadership Potential

(773) 255-4407

Cross-Roads.com

At Crossroads Business Partners, we craft professional, investor-ready **Confidential Information Memorandums (CIMs)**. With 500+ CIMs written, we know how to:

- Highlight your company's strengths and growth potential

- Present financials and operations clearly, without jargon

- Translate EBITDA gains into compelling growth stories

- Deliver polished documents trusted by brokers nationwide

CROSSROADS 

Cross-Roads.com

Business Management Consulting

Whether scaling, preparing for transition, or seeking operational clarity, **Andreas Gfesser** helps entrepreneurs and business owners **build stronger companies** through smarter strategies and disciplined execution.

Through **Crossroads Business Partners**, he delivers the strategic insight and hands-on expertise needed to **optimize performance, increase profitability, and enhance long-term enterprise value.**

Transform Your Business Today

Cross-Roads.com   (773) 255-4407

www.ingramcontent.com/pod-product-compliance
Lightning Source LLC
Chambersburg PA
CBHW051445050726

47593CB00005B/1940